On Training and Performance

"Outstanding ... a technical manual (for actors and directors), an historical document of importance, and a volume that is a delight to read."

Ian Watson, *Rutgers*

"An extremely valuable personal account of Roberta Carreri's process as an actor."

Alison Hodge, *Artistic Director, The Quick and the Dead*

"An excellent book with a unique voice."

Ben Spatz, *University of Huddersfield*

Roberta Carreri is one of acclaimed theatre company Odin Teatret's longest-serving actresses, and the last to be trained by Eugenio Barba himself. In this book she relives the milestones of her professional journey, including:

- her first experiences of street theatre
- the discovery of Asian performance traditions
- pedagogical activities and character creation
- encounters with artists and spectators
- the inception of her solo performances, *Judith* and *Salt*.

Interwoven with rich photographic documentation and a wealth of biographical information, this inspiring handbook reveals the professional secrets of an Odin Teatret actress as well as the story of a life of work, research, and passion.

On Training and Performance
Traces of an Odin Teatret actress

Roberta Carreri

Translated and edited by
Frank Camilleri

LONDON AND NEW YORK

First published 2014
by Routledge
2 Park Square, Milton Park, Abingdon, Oxon OX14 4RN

and by Routledge
711 Third Avenue, New York, NY 10017

Routledge is an imprint of the Taylor & Francis Group, an informa business

Text © 2014 Roberta Carreri

The right of Roberta Carreri to be identified as author of this work has been asserted in accordance with sections 77 and 78 of the Copyright, Designs and Patents Act 1988.

All rights reserved. No part of this book may be reprinted or reproduced or utilised in any form or by any electronic, mechanical, or other means, now known or hereafter invented, including photocopying and recording, or in any information storage or retrieval system, without permission in writing from the publishers.

Trademark notice: Product or corporate names may be trademarks or registered trademarks, and are used only for identification and explanation without intent to infringe.

First published in Italian as *Tracce: Training e storia di un'attrice dell'Odin Teatret*, edited by Francesca Romana Rietti, by Il Principe Costante Edizioni, 2007.

British Library Cataloguing in Publication Data
A catalogue record for this book is available from the British Library

Library of Congress Cataloging in Publication Data
A catalog record for this title has been requested

ISBN: 978-1-138-77999-0 (hbk)
ISBN: 978-1-138-78000-2 (pbk)
ISBN: 978-1-315-76942-4 (ebk)

Typeset in Baskerville by Saxon Graphics Ltd, Derby

To those who loved me

Contents

Foreword by Frank Camilleri — xi
Preface in the form of a letter from Eugenio Barba — xix
Acknowledgements — xxi
Photo credits — xxii

PART I
The story and the training — 1

1 Introduction — 3

2 Milan and some dates — 6

3 Holstebro and Carpignano Salentino — 14

4 The transmission of experience — 20

5 Exercises and principles — 26

6 Slow motion — 29

7 Composition — 32

8 Introversion and extroversion — 37

9 Denmark — 42

10 Geronimo and street theatre — 46

11	Sources of inspiration	53
12	Dialogue with tiredness	58
13	Segmentation	61
14	Being decided	67
15	Thought in action	69
16	Improvisations	78
17	Individual improvisation	83
18	Composing a character	88
19	A little digression into private life	93
20	Marble	98
21	Meeting the Asian masters	102
22	*Judith*	111
23	Notes on improvisation	118
24	The voice in training and in performance	127
25	*Salt*	135
26	Our chronic life	145
27	Metamorphosis	158
28	Photographs: a gallery of characters	162

PART II
The workshop **181**

29 'The Dance of Intentions' 183

PART III
Perspectives **209**

30 A memory not only for and by itself – a note on methodology by Francesca Romana Rietti 211

31 Backward steps – epilogue by Nando Taviani 215

Index 230

Foreword
On time and in visibility: training in context

Frank Camilleri

All aspects of Odin Teatret's practice – the training, the performances, the barters, the publications, the events – are built on foundations that integrate *modus operandi* (way of working) with *modus vivendi* (way of life). Such a confluence of experiences is not unique to Odin. Rather, it is a recurring feature of laboratory theatre in the twentieth century. What is unique to Odin is the longevity and consistency of this coming together of the professional and the personal after half a century of existence. Fifty years, and counting, is a long time. Odin's way of working is indeed not only a way of life but a life(time) itself. In this foreword I look briefly at Odin's history through the lens of time to focus on one of its principal performers, Roberta Carreri.

Times have changed since Eugenio Barba set up Odin Teatret in 1964, and yet the company is as active as ever in creating and touring performances, organising events and producing publications all over the world, especially in Europe and South America, and recently also in China. In a sense, Odin has kept up with the times and seems to remain 'of the time'. However, this does not ring true as an adequate description because of the company's strange, or at least unconventional, relationship with time. Odin Teatret always seems to be slightly 'out-of-synch', ahead or behind, the predominant traits in theatre and society. Odin's story can be narrated in very broad brushstrokes – devoid of nuance and detail but evocative enough for an impressionistic picture – in terms of its relation to time. The three major timeframes I identify below overlap significantly with one other and each phase is in itself constituted of various stages.

In the 1960s and 1970s Odin was ahead of its time, not so much in the component elements of its practice but, rather, in the scale and nature of the fusion of vision, aesthetic, training, organisation and social outreach. This included Barba's incredible foresight to document the work in a form that predates the practice-as-research paradigm by at least a quarter of a century, leading to the hypothesis that Odin contributed, directly or otherwise, to the development of the concept. One of Odin's major offerings in this initial phase was in the field of actor training, drawing from various European and Asian sources. Odin's contribution does not so much lie in the development of a specific technique (like biomechanics, plastiques or neutral mask), but in the *personalisation* of training, a process that is based on principles and which draws on different sources. Whether this lack of a specific technique is due to the eclectic nature of the group's early years (which saw them learning from different masters under Barba's guidance) or to a more pronounced emphasis on making performance (which Barba always prioritised as an aim), it is already possible to see a privileging of a mode that fuses the professional and the personal.

Throughout the 1980s and early 1990s, Odin rode and drove the cusp of the wave of new theatre that had come into increasing prominence in the previous two decades: the culture of group laboratory theatre, especially in continental Europe. Even here, Barba's foresight was in evidence: the setting up of the International School of Theatre Anthropology (ISTA) in 1979 anticipated the surge of interest in interculturalism when it peaked in the 1990s. The publication and success of the first English edition of *A Dictionary of Theatre Anthropology: The Secret Art of The Performer* (1991) reflects the spirit of the times. ISTA was a more formalised model of the workshops and encounters that Odin had been organising regularly since the 1960s. It came about due to a funding opportunity which was eventually adopted and developed as a *cavallo di battaglia* (war horse) to attract institutional funding, but which was also a Trojan horse to enable laboratory work to continue.

In the 2000s, the landscape changed considerably for laboratory-based group theatre, reflecting geopolitical developments in the European Union and the advent of new funding structures that led increasingly to a time-restricted project-oriented culture rather than long term group activity. Although this impacted on nascent laboratory ensemble setups, as a long-standing and respected organisation Odin partook of these opportunities and received EU funding for the 2004 and 2005 ISTA sessions. Furthermore, closer collaboration with academic institutions was both the result of and the catalyst for a more widespread diffusion and acknowledgement of practice-as-research and its attendant links with the publishing industry. In this phase, Odin's work, though still very much prominent in various circles (especially in South America), seems to be 'behind the times' not least because of their historical pedigree, the inevitable ageing of its

Foreword xiii

members, and the constant stream of emergent practices that position Odin as 'retro'. In a recent private correspondence, Barba half-joking described the laboratory as 'anachronistic theatre' to counter the currency of terms such as 'intercultural' and 'postdramatic' that emerge periodically.

However, Odin Teatret's temporal measurement is out-of-synch only if set against metronomic time. In responding and adapting to changing circumstances while still retaining its essence (by which I mean its 'guiding principles'), Odin reflects the organic time of growth, ageing and evolution to a degree rarely paralleled in theatre history. The tick of Odin's internal clock, the pulse of its heartbeat, does not always match the tock of the world's mechanised timekeeping.

Roberta Carreri's work as an actress epitomises much of Odin Teatret, its history as well as its *modus operandi* and *modus vivendi*. Carreri joined Odin in 1974 and, as she claims in the book, she was the last actor to be trained by Barba himself. After her, any new members who joined the group were 'adopted' by one of the performers who were responsible for their education and upkeep. This marks a significant development in Odin's history. Among other things, it is an unequivocal acknowledgement-in-praxis of the actor's responsibility vis-à-vis training that is again suggestive of the personal and the professional. As far as Carreri's narrative is concerned, her positioning at this crossroads means that though she was not there at the beginning when it all started in 1964, she was there at the end of this historic beginning, which is an interesting 'off synch' transitional place to be.

By the time Carreri joined the group Odin was already ten years old, which meant that she arrived at a point when the infrastructure at the ensemble's base in Holstebro, the work approaches in the studio and Odin's international links had been more or less established. This must have been an advantage, enabling the young apprentice to 'hit the ground running', fitting in as far as artistic identity and the day-to-day logistics of Odin were concerned. As we read in the book, this did not make it any easier to integrate within an already formed structure (especially when it came to the language barrier), but she could benefit more on a professional level.

In occupying this crossroads in the group's history, then, Carreri is in a unique position of being (1) recipient, (2) agent, and (3) transmitter of what Odin stands for and its way of doing things, its modus. Over the course of four decades she has, first of all, *received* Odin's way, initially as a student and then as an apprentice performer. Secondly, she has *assimilated, developed* and *shaped* Odin's way as a main performer. Thirdly, she has *transmitted* and *diffused* the Odin way as a teacher as well as an ideator and organiser of Odin Week, which came about in 1989 as a result of a specific personal situation (a pregnancy) and which eventually became a funding and promotional model that is still pursued to this day. Accordingly, I will refer to these three aspects as Carreri's 'roles' in Odin's modus.

The 'Odin way' is a composite of how to do things in the studio and in life. It is a way of living life, professionally and as an individual in the ensemble and beyond, in society. Professionally speaking, the 'Odin way' is not a technique, a system or a method, but very much a personal approach that is inspired by and based on a shared history, which in turn also privileges the individual in being essentially an autodidact. The personal (read 'idiosyncratic') quality of the Odin way, which should more accurately be called 'ways', no doubt accounts for the longevity of the group: it allows individuals to develop and pursue their inclinations while at the same time benefitting from the set-up of an ensemble.

The Odin modus indeed reflects the informed autodidacticism that can be traced to Barba himself and the founding actors, who were inspired and learned, in their own and different ways, from masters like Jerzy Grotowski. Though Odin does not embrace a specific system or method, neither is it quite a 'collective' made up of individuals with different practices because its members share a history and a background, indeed a working life. As Carreri points out in the book, however, neither is it a 'commune' because they do not actually live together and various members have individual projects within the Odin framework that include people outside the group. It is this fusion of the professional and the personal, with all the attendant advantages and tensions of working with the same people for such a long time, which makes their work their life in a literal way.

Similar to the three Odin timeframes I identify above, Carreri's three roles as recipient, agent and transmitter are not exclusive but fuse and flow into each other. Carreri's pedagogy, like that of her colleagues, did not wait until she was 'technically ready' to teach: she started transmitting when she was still learning, and it was the pedagogical process itself that enabled her to achieve technical knowledge and practical wisdom (indeed, in a sense it still does). This is a way of working upon oneself through others which is both an example and an extension of Odin's autodidactic methodology that, informed as it is by various performing and martial arts traditions from the world over, is still essentially centred on individual assimilation, development and elaboration.

In Odin's sense, then, being 'ready' to perform, teach, do, and crucially also live, is not a quantitative factor (the extent of how much you know) but a qualitative one (the nature of what you know): it is one that follows the principles of an organic rather than a metronomic time.

Interestingly, Carreri conceives of her Odin story also in terms of time. She refers to the various phases that have characterised her training since joining Odin as 'seasons'. This nomenclature again indicates an elemental organicity because, as she points out, there is no clear demarcation line between the phases; instead they blend into each other like the changing seasons. Carreri identified the seasons in retrospect, not prescriptively. The following is a paraphrased outline of the description that can be found in the book:

First season: discovering new ways of 'thinking the body' and finding scenic presence through exercises learnt from others.

Second season: developing an individual training, and thereby breaking clichés that had accrued in her work over the years.

Third season: concentrating on the organisation of physical scores, on fixed sequences of actions (scenes and dances) which she developed with the assistance of music and objects.

Fourth season: constructing dramaturgically coherent montages that emerge from 'a kind of existential necessity that concretises itself in a theme'.

What is immediately striking about this articulation of an actress's working process is the personalised, individual nature of the work. Arguably this is most evident in the technical agenda of the second season, but it can be found in the other seasons as well. It is at the heart of the compositionally-oriented third season, and of the quasi-metaphysical impulse that drives the performance agency of the fourth season. The individualised nature of the work can also be found in the content of what she acquired in the first season: the exercises she learned were very much the personal developments of Odin's actors. For example, Carreri mentions specifically Iben Nagel Rasmussen's 'Swiss exercises' and Torgeir Wethal's work on acrobatics, balance and slow motion. This integral mix of the personal and the professional gives a new meaning to phrases such as 'a working life' and 'a professional life'.

Similar to the Odin timeframes I identified above, Carreri's seasons are also out-of-synch with each other. She observes that their duration is not the same: some lasted two years, others more than a decade. Such irregularity reflects the organicity of the process, a time conditioned only by the exigencies of personal growth rather than by the set curriculum of an institution. One wonders if the time of Carreri's fourth season is that of eternity, a perpetual extension of the final phase, or if there is space for a *fifth* season.

If not a discrete fifth phase, the writing of her book certainly marks a temporal dimension in constituting a retrospective account, a looking backwards that is also a working backwards, and therefore has the semblance and characteristics of a 'season'. This reflective dynamic is related to the phenomenon that Nando Taviani writes about in the epilogue of this book under the heading of 'Backward Steps'. It is Carreri's time to tell the story of the visible and invisible aspects that made her the actress she is today.

First published in Italian in 2007 and subsequently revised and updated for various translated editions, Carreri's writing of this book marks an ongoing activity that signals another aspect of her practice that needed formation (training), gestation (development) and publication (performance). A book, especially an artistic autobiography of this kind, epitomises the mix of the personal and the professional. This is particularly the case in the subject matter as well as in the manner in which Carreri has written the book, resisting the option of separating training and performance from life.

As the structure of the book illustrates, it is not possible to separate *modus operandi* from *modus vivendi*. The importance of this integration was very much in evidence during the final stages of the work on this translation, when one of the options was to re-structure the content in a way that foregrounded the training and technical aspects to follow current Anglo-American publication trends in theatre studies. The chapter titles should provide a key for readers interested in a description of the technical parts, but those who want the fuller picture of what sustains and shapes that practice will read the seamless narrative as it swings between, and fuses, life and work. Carreri resisted wrenching the training content from the life narrative in the intentional weave of the book. She was adamant not to present what she called 'a recipe book' because for her (and in the laboratory modus of Odin) the exercises are just the visible aspect in the formation of an actor. Training, technique and craft are all essential, but they are just a part of the story rather than the story itself. They are the tip of an iceberg whose mass is submerged and invisible below sea level. In turn, even this tip is submerged during the act of performance.

The chapter in Part Two on the workshop, entitled 'The Dance of Intentions', was Carreri's response to the publishing industry's need to highlight the technical aspect of her work. The same applies to the slight alteration in the title of the English edition, which gives prominence to training but at the same time is intended to reflect the laboratory tradition's incorporation of 'life' in the 'art' of the performer. Carreri undertook the challenge of putting into words what till then had been a lived pedagogical experience for her. This new addition, written specifically for the English version, gives readers an invaluable glimpse into not only the most visible features of Carreri's training (i.e. some of her exercises), but also what drives and structures that work. It is like a window on the decision-making, the strategic patterns and options available to an experienced actress in a pedagogical situation, what in another age we could have called 'the artist's mind at work'. It is necessary to signal the importance of this new chapter because such insight in the logic behind technical and craft choices is not always immediately accessible when one observes or participates in a workshop.

The fusion of the personal and professional in Carreri's authorial position reflects an integration of aesthetics with ethics. In an article on performer training in the twenty-first century, I argue that there are ethical and ideological approaches to actor training, with the former marking a more holistic and organic approach, and the latter indicating institutionalised forms of training.[1] The professional/life processes of learning, transmission and performance that Carreri has experienced is a reflection of the ethical approach.

Although there is no short cut or fast formula, taken in isolation, the essential elements in Carreri's approach are simple. However, it is a deceptive simplicity if the tip of that particular iceberg is not sustained by something other than the capacity and ability to execute exercises. The tasks themselves, which are inspired from various sources ranging from games to Asian techniques to photographs, could have taken a different shape. However, it is individual commitment that drives these technically doable exercises. The learning process occurs not so much in the assimilation of codified forms as in the engagement and persistence of the task-activity itself. The simplicity of this approach also signals its difficulty because it sets one against personal limits, and it does so on one's own terms, which is arguably the most difficult thing to do. It is a work upon oneself, however mediated or facilitated it may be by the teacher.

Carreri's approach, which embodies the personalisation of training, reminds me of the advice Ingemar Lindh once gave me as an aspiring performer in the mid-1990s: to do what you want to do in life. It is revealing that Lindh replied to a technical and professional question about actor training with an answer concerning 'life'. It is such simple advice, and yet it is probably the hardest to achieve because there are no set paths to follow and there are always concerns and demands and excuses that come in the way. Again, the difficulty of this advice is that it sets you up against yourself.

It is not a coincidence that Carreri herself begins her narrative in this book with a reference to Lindh on technique. She quotes his image of the visually beautiful snow that covers the iron underneath: 'Technique is like an iron staircase, cold and hard but necessary. When it snows it becomes white, soft, and shining. In performances, spectators should see the snow and not the staircase'. The connection between doing-in-life and doing-in-the-studio is indeed in many ways a work upon oneself, a personal reconfiguration of vision and time, of a life lived.

Note

1 Frank Camilleri, 'Of Pounds of Flesh and Trojan Horses: Performer Training in the Twenty-first Century', *Performance Research*, 14:2 (2009), 26–34.

Preface in the form of a letter
from Eugenio Barba

Dear Roberta,

We live cloistered in skies of words, ideas, stories and conventions. Beneath these skies floats an island we call theatre. We can inhabit this island either as a haven or as a place where we can stand on tiptoe in order to tear, here and there, the veils of those skies in the hope of glimpsing the point of contact joining the two worlds between which we balance: the world of illusions that help us to live and the world of reality which some of us cannot bear to gaze at for long.

If I knew how to draw, I would not have written anything for your book but I would have sent you a picture of these skies, and within them our theatre, and you within our theatre. Worlds within worlds, with the double urge to seek protection in them and to lacerate them.

Many years ago you presented yourself on the doorstep of our theatre like a little Friday cast up on Robinson Crusoe's island. I do not remember if you explained your *true* reasons, what you were *really* escaping from or what you were seeking. I just asked myself a practical question: were we prepared to accept and take care of you? Yes, we were. In a more or less direct manner, I also asked you an equally practical question: were you prepared to stay? You were. Then I said to myself: let's see if she holds out. In our theatre no one recruits and no one is recruited. One tries. Then, as a result of trying, something binds in the relationship until there is the certainty – perhaps true, perhaps illusory – of an indissoluble bond.

For many months and years you were a Friday to whom everything had to be taught: how to move and make your voice heard, how to model your presence. We call it 'technique'. But we know very well that it is a way of changing one's life in a concrete fashion, showing through deeds one's own impatience and unexpressed hopes. With the tools of the craft and without many words.

Now, instead of watching you physically at work, I leaf through the pages of your book and read your words.

I am sure that with the passing of the years you are aware of my pride at seeing you become independent, an actress capable of inventing her own way, a student who has become a master. I am filled with pride when the moment arrives in which I no longer have to teach anything, and we can work together to build something which neither of us anticipates and which will become a new performance. I think you can easily imagine this pride, even when I do not show you the signs.

But I believe it cannot be easy for you to imagine the pride that I feel when faced with your book. I feel that pride deeply every time one of you, actresses and actors of Odin Teatret, writes and publishes something. When I look at your book, I say to myself: not only have you acquired independence as an actress, but you have also achieved it on an intellectual level. It is almost always the others who write about actors: the spectator-critics, the historians, the professional intellectuals; and directors often speak on their behalf.

When you actors manage to master *your own* words, *your own* way of formulating, narrating, transmitting and remembering, our island becomes not only more precious and diverse but also more just.

It is beautiful to see these paper flowers blossom, where an essential part of our life finds words which are always different depending on the people who have had the ability to write them. You have worked hard on this book, just as you do in the room where you train, creating material and rehearsing performances, some of which are new and some you have been doing for years. Even after all this time and so many experiences, finding the necessary pattern of a movement is not easy for you, but it is familiar. However, it cannot have been easy, without sounding inadequate or deceitful, to find the right words which did not shrivel the passion and tacit knowledge, reducing them to banalities.

I am sure that the deleted words have been more numerous than the ones which have remained. More than once you must have said to yourself: it's not worth it, I'm going to stop. But this time, too, you did not give up.

The skies will darken. Gossip and oblivion will prevail among distorted memories and amputated stories. No one can predict whether your words, today still fresh from the press, will succeed in transmitting some of their truth. But this should not bother you. That which had to be done, you have done. The rest does not belong to you.

Holstebro, 23 October 2006

Acknowledgements

Thanks to Teatro Tascabile di Bergamo for providing the theatre space in which the photographic documentation of my work demonstration *Traces in the Snow* could take place.

Thanks to Eugenio Barba, Teresa Cancellieri, Sosi Enzi, Raúl Iaiza, Tina Nielsen, Mirella Schino, Nando Taviani and Torgeir Wethal for reading my pages and for helping me with their comments and advice.

Thanks to Claudio Coloberti, Ana Sofia Monsalve and Rina Skeel for their collaboration in the digitisation of photographic material.

Thanks to Guendalina Ravazzoni for her precious photographic documentation of *Traces in the Snow*.

Thanks to Fiora Bemporad, Tony D'Urso, Torben Huss, Jan Rüsz, Luca Ruzza, Saul Shapiro, Rina Skeel and Torgeir Wethal for allowing me to make use of their photographs.

Thanks to Francesca Romana Rietti, my fellow traveller.

Thanks to Sarah Dey Hirshan, Glenn Hall, Nick Slie and Emily Ayres for their precious suggestions to the English version.

And finally, thanks to Vanessa Chizzini and Valeria Ravera for spurring me on to write this book.

Photo credits

Roberta Carreri Archive: pp. 16, 22, 49, 96
Fiora Bemporad: p. 178 (bottom)
Tony D'Urso: pp. 17, 47, 50, 162, 163, 164 (top and bottom left), 165, 167, 168, 169, 170, 171, 176, 177
Torben Huss: p. 94
Guendalina Ravazzoni: pp. 31, 32, 33, 34, 35, 36, 38, 39, 40, 56, 62, 66, 73, 74, 75, 76, 77, 80, 81, 82, 87, 90, 91, 103, 104, 105, 106, 107, 108, 113, 132, 133
Jan Rüsz: pp. 166, 172, 173, 174, 175
Luca Ruzza: p. 178 (top)
Saul Shapiro: p. 164 (bottom right)
Rina Skeel: p. 44, 179
Torgeir Wethal: p. 43

Part I
The story and the training

1 Introduction

Ingemar Lindh once told me: 'Technique is like an iron staircase, cold and hard but necessary. When it snows it becomes white, soft, and shining. In performances, spectators should see the snow and not the staircase'.[1]

This is the reason why I called the work demonstration which I created in 1988 *Traces in the Snow*. *Traces* stand for technical signs (a way of training which others can follow), and *snow* represents my scenic presence in the situations where I manifest those signs.

In 2004 Vanessa Chizzini and Valeria Ravera from the publishing house Il Principe Costante saw my work demonstration at the Teatro della Madrugada in Milan. A year later they asked me to transpose *Traces in the Snow* into a written text. They were willing to publish it accompanied by photographs.

In *Traces in the Snow* I narrate my artistic biography from 1974 to 1987. I follow a chronological thread, tracing the development of my training and the creation of some of my characters. I narrate the story by highlighting the salient points, illustrating it with practical examples. My demonstration lasts only two hours, but in this book I can enrich it with new details, examples and episodes, as well as update it to 2012.

There will be moments in my narrative when, for the sake of chronology, I skip from training situations to the birth of a character. In other instances I will leap back and forth in time because different events occurring simultaneously and along parallel paths are obliged to follow a linear progression once they are transcribed onto paper.

When I decided to abandon my life in Milan to join Odin Teatret, I chose also to flee from the ambiguity of words. I preferred to confront myself through action in silence rather than rely on words that were not backed by deeds.

4   *The story and the training*

Now, thirty-eight years later, I find myself once again confronting words in an endeavour to translate my experiences into written signs, in the process engaging with the difficulty of having to describe effectively what I now know how to do in practice.

Theatre is a craft and as such it cannot simply be learnt in books. Technique is transmitted by means of practical examples. However, books can be a source of inspiration. I know of people who have built their individual work practice after reading and interpreting written works.

For over forty years Odin Teatret has grown like a medieval city, in various directions according to the needs of the moment. Thus there will be many aspects that will not be covered in this book, such as the story of Odin Teatret in its historical context, its economic structure, descriptions of its performances, the barter exchanges, the tours, the Festuger in Holstebro and all the other activity in the community that emerges from it,[2] the workshops, Odin Week, the publication of books and journals, the production of films and audio-video material, and the network of contacts that generates the microcosm in which we move with our activities.

I will not attempt to reconstruct Eugenio Barba's method of creating performances, if there is such a method. In this book you will not find any portraits of my fellow actors. There is a simple reason for this. The theme of *Traces* is the actor's training as I have experienced it, and its influence on the creation of characters in performances.

I have agreed to write this book so that my experience can serve as an inspiration for those people (now and in the future) who are drawn to this way of living the theatre, and to make some of those who are already living it in this way feel less alone.

This text is another step in the tradition of transmission of experience that has characterised the story of Odin Teatret ever since the beginning, and of which the work demonstrations are a key factor.

Notes

1   Ingemar Lindh was a Swedish actor, director, pedagogue and mime. In 1972 he founded the Institutet för Scenkonst in Storhögen, Sweden. From 1966 to 1968 he was a pupil of Étienne Decroux at his school in Boulogne-Billancourt. From 1968 to 1970 he formed part of the atelier Studio 2 founded by Yves Lebreton in 1968 and hosted, as an independent entity, by Odin Teatret until 1973. Lindh was also one of the founders of ISTA, and he participated, as a pedagogue, in the second session held in Volterra in 1981. In 1995 he co-founded the research programme xHCA (*questioning* Human Creativity as Acting) at the University of Malta. Ingemar Lindh died in 1997.

2 'Festuger' is the Danish word for 'celebration week'. Every three years since 1991 Odin Teatret organises a Festuge in Holstebro. For seven days and nights the town is 'invaded' by local and visiting groups and artists who, in association with the local cultural institutions, hold theatre and dance performances (inside and outdoors), concerts, barters, conferences and exhibitions, as well as visiting schools, old people's homes, shops and government buildings.

2 Milan and some dates

Milan, 1944: Fausto Carreri and Ada Papotti meet on tram 23 which still runs from the neighbourhood of Città Studi to Piazza Fontana to this day. Both of them were living with their families in Città Studi after moving from the Mantovan countryside before the outbreak of war. They were married in 1946 and seven years later, on the 29th of June 1953, I, Roberta Barbara Carreri, was born.

My father was a specialised worker at the Alfa Romeo factory and my mother a housewife. At home we spoke Mantovan dialect. When I started school my mother assisted some relatives who had a shop. I spent the afternoons playing with other children in the streets.

The Leonardo da Vinci primary school, in the square of the same name, had an underground swimming pool where we learnt to swim. In the third year of primary school we were offered the opportunity to learn English after school hours. Our teacher was a native speaker and she took great pains to make us pronounce the English *th* and *t* sounds properly. My father's dream was that one day I would become an air hostess, speaking many languages and travelling around the world. My dream was to become a dancer.

When I received a pair of red silk ballet shoes as a gift, I tiptoed all over the apartment. I fantasised about being accepted at the ballet school of Teatro Alla Scala. I was told that even girls from a poor background could make it: the famous ballerina Carla Fracci was a tram driver's daughter, after all. In the meantime, my father had been promoted to section foreman.

In photographs from those days I am as skinny as a stick, dressed in shorts and with my hair cut like a boy. My nickname was Biafra. Healthwise, I was delicate, anaemic and lymphatic. Every spring the family doctor prescribed a dose of vitamin B, and every summer the sea was obligatory.

After having regularly saved up from a meagre salary, the summer holidays in rented rooms with shared kitchens were my mother's coveted reward. I spent the other two months of the holidays with my relatives in the Mantovan countryside, where in the mornings I was given roasted quails and egg yolk laced with a spot of China Martini.[1] At five years of age I was given my first *ronchinin* with which I could join in the grape harvest.[2]

When I was eleven years old my father was diagnosed with tuberculosis and had to spend a year in hospital. To make up for my father's reduced salary my mother rented my room to an engineering student and I slept in her room.

On his return from hospital, my father was re-trained by Alfa Romeo and was then transferred to an office job. My family moved to another house in Città Studi that had a lift, because after his illness my father was frequently out of breath from climbing five flights of stairs. The new house had one room missing compared with the previous one: mine.

At the end of secondary school I had to choose between art or graphic design. We chose the latter because it meant that I could find a job earlier. This is how I ended up at the Caterina da Siena professional state institute for girls, where I was fortunate enough to have Renzo Vescovi as a lecturer of Italian and history as well as a life teacher.[3] In class he instilled in us a love for Manzoni, and we discussed articles from *L'Espresso*.[4] He introduced us to Molière and had us read Heidegger, Kant, Sartre and Camus. Although he was always formal in his manners, he taught us to think for ourselves and to take responsibility for our choices.

The student revolts of 1968 were also felt in our institute of 1200 girls between the ages of fifteen and eighteen. I soon became one of the most militant activists of the student movement. Demonstrations, protest marches, and tear gas.

Saturday afternoons were passed at the discotheque and Sundays at the art house cinema or at the theatre. At the Teatro Lirico, during the interval of *Saint Joan of the Stockyards* directed by Giorgio Strehler I met Beppe Chierichetti, a chemical engineering student who became my boyfriend and later an actor of the Teatro Tascabile di Bergamo.

I received my diploma in graphic design and a year later I sat for my final examination. If I passed I would become the first person in my family ever to enter university. During the day I answered the telephone for a little firm. At night I studied.

In 1972 I registered at the Faculty of Literature and Philosophy at the Università Statale di Milano. My parents beamed with pride. In the mornings I worked as a page-setter for a financial magazine, and in the afternoons I attended classes and reading groups. The evenings were passed either taking part in the meetings of the Comitati Unitari di Base (part of the far left-wing organisation Avanguardia Operaia) or studying Hindi.

My aim was to graduate in Art Criticism, but destiny had a surprise in store.

In the spring of 1973 Renzo Vescovi hosted *Min Fars Hus*, an Odin Teatret performance by Eugenio Barba, at the Teatro Tascabile di Bergamo.[5] 'An occasion not to be missed,' said Renzo when I bumped into him in the cloister of the University where I was studying and he was lecturing in the history of Italian literature. It was a fortunate coincidence, because at the time I was preparing for an examination that included texts by Artaud, Grotowski and Barba.

I had been frequenting the Milan theatres for the previous four years, and on that May evening, as our car clambered up towards Bergamo, I was convinced that I was about to see a good performance. We parked the car at the entrance of the beautiful medieval piazza where the Teatro Tascabile had its base. The air was warm and gentle. The little foyer was full of people and its lights brought out the colours of our spring clothes.

The performance was limited to sixty spectators only. I was among the first to get in. The floor had been covered with wooden boards which suffused the air with an unusual smell. One metre away from the wall, a rectangle of benches was festooned with electric bulbs. My skin reacted with a shudder to the temperature, which was perceptibly lower than outside. All the spectators were seated on the benches when the actors walked in.

I remember writing the following words some days after the event:

> *A daisy between toes. A voice and a name: Fyodor Dostoyevsky. Then the sound of an accordion playing music. Dancing. Beer flowing down the necks, falling and soaking the wood. Smell. Darkness. Silence. Voices. A little flame illuminates a flower, a glass of water, and the face of a young woman lying on the floor held up by a colleague.*
>
> *And then even more music and lights and dancing, endlessly. Meetings. Clashes. Embraces. Darkness. Candle flames reveal long hair stuck with sweat around burning faces.*
>
> *The air becomes stiflingly hot. I lose every sensation of my body. I can only feel my burning cheeks.*
>
> *A big piece of black cloth covers the space and falls on the floor.*

A man, on his feet, blindfolded, in a shirt, laughs hysterically while a young man with long blond hair and with a coat around his shoulders falls repeatedly under a hail of coins. The man removes the blindfold, the eyes meet and the looks fuse into each other. A moment of beauty that hurts. An embrace, the coat covers the shoulders of both men.

My eyes brim with tears as the music carries the actors away with it, leaving us on our own in the heavy air of consummated passions.

I sat still as the other spectators made their exit. I uncrossed my legs, which I had not moved for the entire performance, and ran to the small dark passage between the hall and the dressing rooms. There I cried for a long time. I wept because of the emotions provoked in me by all the energy, all the beauty, all the vitality in those seven shining bodies.

It was a kind of energy and vitality that belonged also to my childhood when I had run about in the streets with other children, where the rules of honour and loyalty were physical. You were what you did. Throwing stones or breathless races, pissing against the wall (including me, the only girl, who did not feel any different in my shorts and tomboy hair). And then there were the denunciations, the fights, the gestures of generosity, the joy of speaking to each other again after days of proud silence. That is where I learned about loyalty and friendship.

My days in the streets came to an end with the beginning of secondary school. My mother told me that it was about time I stopped spending my afternoons in via Bazzini, because I was a girl and I should begin to act like one. I had to play inside like all the other girls.

Ten years had passed since then, and when I saw *Min Fars Hus* the energy which was unleashed from those bodies hit me like the taste of Proust's famous *madeleine*: 'A fascination which poured out and overflowed and shook the essence of existence itself.'

The following morning I returned to Bergamo. In the same space where the performance had taken place the previous evening, Iben Nagel Rasmussen[6] and Jens Christensen,[7] under the guidance of Eugenio Barba, demonstrated their training to a group of observers. During the discussion that ensued I was not surprised when one of my fellow students accused them of being elitist. At the time it was unthinkable to present a performance for just sixty spectators. Furthermore, regardless of the colourful clothes they wore, the actors' training seemed to demand a military kind of discipline. The student movement of 1968 had been, in part, a revolt against discipline.

10   *The story and the training*

In December 1973 Odin Teatret returned to Italy for the Triennale di Milano with *Min Fars Hus*. I participated in the workshop they held at the Università Cattolica.

I arrived for the workshop terrified of having to do the headstands and other acrobatic exercises which I had seen Iben and Jens doing earlier that year. Instead I danced for hours to the music of Janis Joplin and the Rolling Stones (something which I loved doing). The theme of the workshop, conducted by Eugenio Barba and five of his actors, was energy: it turned out to be a veritable dance marathon. Eugenio had the participants take it in turns to sit out and then rejoin the dancing to see how an exhausted group would react to the intervention of a freshly rested person.

At the end of the first day I had big blisters on the soles of my feet. On the following day those blisters burst during the dancing, but the pain did not diminish my enthusiasm. I remember dancing nonstop with Tage Larsen all through Janis Joplin's album *Pearl* and then to the entire Rolling Stones' *Gimme Shelter*.[8] At the end we exchanged a sincere hand-kiss.

On the final day of the workshop I had lunch with them. Then I spent the afternoon walking around the city with Ragnar Christiansen.[9]

After the Milan performances, Odin Teatret returned once again to Bergamo to present *Min Fars Hus* at the Teatro Tascabile.

I bought a Christmas hamper full of fruit and wine for the actors and went to see the performance again. I wanted to relive the experience of the first time, but this time I could not help recognising, beneath their costumes, the actors with whom I had done the workshop. After the performance I accepted their invitation to go with the group to La Marianna, a nearby restaurant. I sat at a table with Ragnar, Jens, Torgeir[10] and Iben.

When I saw Else Marie[11] coming out of the theatre, wearing glasses and wrapped in a fur coat, I mistook her for the group secretary. Now she was sitting at another table with Ulrik[12] and Tage, the latter wearing a wide-brimmed black hat. It did not take long for Ragnar to disappear behind a pyramid of Sambuca glasses and become melancholic. For my part, emboldened by a cognac offered by Torgeir, I embarked on the reckless venture of translating some poems by Eugenio Montale into English. Ulrik came over to our table and taught me my first words of Danish: '*Og hvad nu?*' (And now what?).

Eugenio and Torgeir returned to Italy some months later in April 1974. They were looking for a space to house the group for five months so they could focus on the creation of a new performance. On their way to Puglia, where they had been offered the possibility of a residence, they stopped at the Piccolo Teatro di Pontedera to show the films on the training of Odin Teatret, which Torgeir had produced for the experimental programmes of the Italian national television station Rai Tre.

The Teatro Tascabile di Bergamo went to Pontedera to see the film, and I, in the guise of Beppe's girlfriend, went with them.

In the garden of the seventeenth-century villa where the Piccolo Teatro di Pontedera had its base, I ran into a young man I had met in Milan some years earlier at one of the performances of Teatro del Trebbo. At that time he had been serving his sixteen month obligatory military service, but wearing a uniform and having his head shaved did not reduce the brightness of his eyes. It was Roberto Bacci, the director of the Piccolo Teatro di Pontedera whose *Macbeth* we were about to see that evening.

After the performance I asked Eugenio for an appointment on the following day. He surprised me when he addressed me by name. How did he remember? I wanted his advice on my intention to write a thesis on the work of Odin Teatret. I had already found the title: *From the Body as Statue to the Body as Music*. The following day Eugenio told me that to really know the work process of Odin Teatret I had to take part in a performance. Two years were required: one for rehearsals and another for touring. I had to co-ordinate with Iben to figure out the best time to visit them in Denmark.

I left for Holstebro, telling my parents that I had been invited by Odin Teatret to participate in a week-long workshop on Balinese theatre (although I was well aware that the workshop would have ended by the time I arrived), and that both travel and accommodation were paid for.[13] Instead I used the money I had set aside in case I ever needed an abortion, which could be had in England at that time.

Notes

1 China Martini is made from the bark of the China Calissaia (Chinaroot), a tree originating high in the Andean mountains of Peru and Bolivia. From the eighth century, a fine digestive liqueur was produced in China based on an infusion made of Chinaroot bark and rice alcohol.
2 In the Mantovan dialect 'ronchinin' is the term for a small sickle used to separate the grape bunch from the vine.
3 Renzo Vescovi was the director of the Teatro Tascabile di Bergamo – Accademia delle Forme Sceniche, which he founded in 1973. In 1977 the Teatro Tascabile di Bergamo began researching street-theatre techniques, eventually becoming one of its major exponents in Europe. The Teatro Tascabile's 1977 encounter with the Odissi dancer Aloka Paniker left an important mark on the history of the group. Since then, after having founded

12 The story and the training

the Institute of Oriental Scenic Culture (IXO), the Tascabile actors embarked on a long process of apprenticeship in Indian dance practices (specifically Odissi and Kathakali) with frequent residential study visits to India under the guidance of various teachers. Renzo Vescovi died in 2005.

4   L'Espresso is one of the two most prominent Italian weeklies. It enjoys the reputation of being the main politically independent news magazine in Italy.

5   Min Fars Hus (My Father's House), 1972–74. A performance dedicated to Fyodor Dostoyevsky. Actors: Jens Christensen, Ragnar Christiansen, Malou Illmoni (who left the group after the first weeks of performances), Tage Larsen, Else Marie Laukvik, Iben Nagel Rasmussen, Ulrik Skeel and Torgeir Wethal. Adaptation and direction by Eugenio Barba.

6   Iben Nagel Rasmussen is a Danish actress who has been with Odin Teatret since 1966. She has performed in all the group performances with the exception of The Gospel According to Oxyrhincus (1985–87). She also performs in Itsi Bitsi (1991–present, adapted and directed by Eugenio Barba) together with Kai Berdholt and Jan Ferslev as actor-musicians. Since 1976 she has been developing an autonomous pedagogical work with a group of actors who, despite operating in different contexts and countries, manage to get together periodically to work on shared research interests. She founded her first group, Farfa, in 1980. In 1989 she launched Vindenes Bro (The Bridge of Winds) and, more recently, De Nye Vinde (New Winds), both of which are still active. In 2006 Rasmussen presented Ester's Book, a performance based on a text she wrote herself and with scenic advice from Eugenio Barba. She is accompanied on the violin by Uta Motz in the Danish version of the performance and by Elena Floris in the Italian.

7   Jens Christensen, a Danish actor who worked with Odin Teatret from 1970 to 1974. He performed in the group performance Min Fars Hus.

8   Tage Larsen is a Danish actor who has been with Odin Teatret since 1971. After a brief pause in 1974 he remained with the group until 1987 when he founded Yorik Teatret. Larsen returned to Odin Teatret in 1997. He has participated in all the group performances since 1971 except Talabot and Kaosmos.

9   Ragnar Christiansen, a Norwegian actor who worked with Odin Teatret from 1970 to 1974. He performed in the group performance Min Fars Hus.

10 Torgeir Wethal was a Norwegian actor who had been with Odin Teatret since its inception in 1964. He was the only actor who acted in all the group performances until 2010. Wethal was also the producer of Odin Teatret Film, and directed various films and documentaries on the performance and pedagogical work of Odin Teatret and other twentieth-century theatre traditions. He died of lung cancer in June 2010.

11 Else Marie Laukvik, a Norwegian actress who was with Odin Teatret since its inception in 1964, is still involved with the group. Her last performance under the direction of Eugenio Barba was Memoria (1990–92) where she was accompanied by Frans Winther, musician and composer with Odin Teatret. From 1964 to 1990 she took part in all the group performances except Brecht's Ashes and Talabot. She has developed an autonomous research activity as founder and director of Teatro Marques in Aarhus for more than ten years. Laukvik is still involved in various pedagogical projects with other groups and students.

12 Ulrik Skeel is a Danish actor who worked with Odin Teatret from 1969 to 1974 and then from 1978 to 1987. Since 1988 he has worked with the administrative staff of the theatre.
13 Holstebro is a small city in Danish Jutland. Odin Teatret moved from Oslo to Holstebro in 1966, and it is still based there today.

3 Holstebro and Carpignano Salentino

I arrived in Holstebro on 24 April 1974 at midnight after travelling for twenty-five hours by train. I was tired and excited. Iben and Torgeir took me to a little hotel in front of the train station. They picked me up the following morning at six to take me to the theatre, where the work started at seven. I was surprised to see that the *Min Fars Hus* ensemble had dissolved; only Iben, Jens, Ragnar and Torgeir remained from the performers I had seen in Bergamo.

From the second day, my education was entrusted to Jens. We started at five in the morning with a run, after which we practised acrobatics and then exercises with sticks. When Eugenio and the others arrived at seven we continued the training together and then worked on improvisations for the new performance. Jens also introduced me to the unwritten rules of the group. Today I remember the one that prohibited Odin Teatret members from having intimate relationships with each other (at the time I was not aware that this rule had already been broken) and the one that forbade us from making any comments on the work of the other actors, whether inside or outside the working space.

It was my intention to stay for a week only so I could get a glimpse of how Odin Teatret worked and to breathe some of their air. So I was quite surprised at the attention they dedicated to my formation, making me work hard from five in the morning to six in the evening.

When I mentioned to Eugenio that I was returning to Milan in three days' time, he was very surprised and said, 'But you are now part of Odin!' It was my turn to be surprised. In Milan I had my parents, Beppe, university, friends and a political commitment. No. I did not feel I could change my life like this, point blank.

From that moment I was allowed to keep training with Jens from five to seven in the morning, but I was prohibited from entering the space when the actors worked with Eugenio. In the solitude of the theatre's big library I had a lot of time to rethink my decision. Two days later I knocked on the door of Eugenio's office. 'If I manage to sort out my things in Milan, can I join you in Salento'?[1] 'If God wills it we'll meet again', he said without turning his head.

On my return to Milan I spoke to my parents, reached an agreement with my university professors, sought the advice of Renzo Vescovi who told me not to leave, and discussed the matter with Beppe Chierichetti who backed my decision. After all, it was only for a year or two. I could study from Holstebro, researching for my thesis, and return to Milan to take my examinations.

'Odin Teatret, Carpignano Salentino.' This was the address I had in my hands when I left Milan on 18 May 1974.

I could not find Carpignano Salentino on the map, but I knew that it was somewhere near Lecce. In any case the train could not take me further than that. On the train I asked a young woman who was sitting in the same compartment if she knew of a place where I could spend the night in Lecce. I did not know the city, I had little money, and I was afraid of ending up in some shady guesthouse or other. She was very friendly and said that an acquaintance of hers could probably host me; she gave me a name and an address and suggested that I tell her friend that we worked together in Milan.

The house was in the old part of the city. The old lady who opened the door lived with her older sister, both of whom seemed like characters from a fairy tale: one could not hear and the other could not see. They treated me suspiciously. I told them the story that the woman in the train had suggested, but they remained reticent. Then the telephone rang, and from the old lady's voice I understood that she was talking to someone very important to her. When she hung up the receiver she turned to me with a respectful smile. That night she gave me her bed. I tried to insist that I could sleep on the sofa, but to no avail. The following morning I bought a bunch of flowers for the two sisters and then scouted for information about how to proceed with my journey.

Strangely enough, nobody could tell me how to reach Carpignano. Of course there was a bus – but from where did it depart? 'Try further that way.' 'Try on the other side of the street.' It felt like I was in a foreign country. I was wandering about in the vicinity of the train station with my rucksack on my shoulders and the sun directly on top of me when, from the hot opaque air, the colourful figures of Iben and Torgeir emerged. I cried out with joy.

'God willed it,' Eugenio told me, his eyes smiling from behind the dark circles of his glasses. Nando Taviani was sitting next to him in the lobby of the Grand Hotel of Lecce. When Nando shook my hand I had the odd feeling that he knew me already. Later I learnt that he was a university professor in Theatre History and that he was responsible for the collaborative project between the University of Lecce and Odin Teatret. He had helped Eugenio find the space where the group was about to work for the next five months.

I woke up before sunrise, at five in the morning; the thought of another day of suffering made me feel like throwing up. Nevertheless, I jumped on my bicycle and covered the two kilometres that separated the castle of Serrano, where I was sleeping, and the castle of Carpignano, where the majority of my companions were staying and where most of our activities were taking place. From there we walked towards the tobacco fields or the seashore for vocal training. Then, as the sun was rising, we went running. On our return to the castle we had a frugal breakfast, after which we worked until eleven on physical training and with objects (sticks and wands of various sizes, decorated with ribbons). At this point we had a lunch break as the heat became unbearable in the old disused tobacco factory where we worked.

In the courtyard of Carpignano Salentino's castle (1974). From left: Jens Christensen, Odd Ström, Roberta Carreri, Iben Nagel Rasmussen, Torgeir Wethal and Elsa Kvamme.

Roberta Carreri training in the courtyard of Carpignano Salentino's castle (1974).

I was confronted every day with running, physical exercises that were very hard for me, and acrobatic leaps that my body could not do. My body was aching all over. In the early afternoon, while the others were resting, Eugenio observed my work with the 'little torches' (two small sticks with tufts of coloured strips of fabric at the end) and he patiently helped me to construct a dramatic dance with them. After I had only been in the group for two months the dramatisation of our training with these kinds of objects led to the creation of *The Book of Dances*,[2] my first performance. After four p.m., when the sun lost some of its intensity, my companions would come back and we would work on the new performance *Come! And the Day Will Be Ours*.[3]

After half a year, from the eight actors who had been in the white room in April 1974,[4] only Torgeir, Iben and I remained. Else Marie and Tage rejoined the group in 1975.

During my first year with Odin Teatret it was not encouraging to see so many companions leave. The most difficult moment was undoubtedly in August after the holidays. In the courtyard of Carpignano castle, Jens, with his hair and beard shaved, told us of his decision to leave the group to become a farmer in Norway. It was the first time that I saw Eugenio cry.

During our stay in Carpignano, Eugenio also directed the first clown performance in Odin Teatret's history, *Johann Sebastian Bach* with Jan Torp,[5] Odd Ström[6] and Iben Nagel Rasmussen. In the final scene I would make an appearance in the guise of a 'victim'. Dressed in a tartan miniskirt, heeled shoes and an immaculate blouse (my clothes from Milan), I was 'fished' out from the audience by Jan, taken on stage, tied to a chair and wrapped up in a length of white cloth. I was then given the 'barber' treatment: Odd used a broom to throw foam on my face from a tub while Jan shaved my 'beard' with an enormous wooden razor. It all ended with an 'egg shampoo' performed by Jan, who broke two fresh eggs on my head as the audience went into raptures of delight.

I had arrived at Odin Teatret directly from my parents' house where I had never cooked anything in my life. At Carpignano we took turns to cook, so when my turn came I called my mother (using all my money on long-distance phone calls) for some recipes.

Danish and Norwegian were spoken at the table as well as in the theatre, but both were unknown languages for me. When my companions laughed at a joke I looked around, not knowing what to do.

I woke up every morning with the thought of leaving the theatre that day. As I washed and got dressed I thought of the words that I would say to Eugenio. While I had breakfast and rode my bicycle I thought of the things I would do on my return to Milan. But the moment I met Eugenio and the others, this internal dialogue was silenced. I did what I was told, and before I knew it, it was the evening.

I had left the city where I was born, where I had family, friends, companions and a boyfriend to remind me of who I was. Now I had to relearn how to speak, move and sing in addition to learning, from scratch, how to cook. I had to build a new identity among persons who did not know me and with whom I had nothing in common, except the desire to live our dreams working with Eugenio Barba.

Holstebro and Carpignano Salentino   19

It took years to dismantle my 'Milanese identity'. Then, like a phoenix, I was reborn from the ashes.

Notes

1 In April 1974 Odin Teatret was about to depart for Carpignano Salentino, in Puglia (Italy), for five months of work and research.
2 *The Book of Dances*, 1974–80, presented indoors but mainly outside, was the performance with which Odin Teatret accomplished its first theatre barters. Actors (in the version presented in 1974 in Salento): Roberta Carreri, Elsa Kvamme, Iben Nagel Rasmussen, Odd Ström and Torgeir Wethal. From 1975 onwards, Elsa Kvamme and Odd Ström were replaced by Tom Fjordefalk, Tage Larsen and Else Marie Laukvik. Direction: Eugenio Barba.
3 *Come! And the Day Will Be Ours*, 1976–80. Actors: Roberta Carreri, Tom Fjordefalk, Tage Larsen, Else Marie Laukvik, Iben Nagel Rasmussen and Torgeir Wethal. Dramaturgy and direction: Eugenio Barba.
4 At the time there were two work spaces at Odin Teatret, named after the colour of their walls: 'the black room' (the first to be built during the renovations that transformed the environs of an empty farmhouse, offered by the local council of Holstebro to Odin Teatret in 1966 and which still serves as its base) and the 'white room', built in 1968. Two other rooms were constructed over the course of time: the 'red' in 1980 and the 'blue' in 1986.
5 Jan Torp, a Danish man who worked at Odin Teatret in lieu of military service, later joined the group as tour manager and technician. In 1974, after taking part in a workshop of the Colombaioni brothers organised by Odin Teatret in Holstebro and acting as a stooge for Romano Colombaioni on tour in Denmark, he created two clown performances with Odin Teatret: *Johann Sebastian Bach* and *Saltimbanchi e Spaghetti*. He left the group in 1978.
6 Odd Ström, a Norwegian actor who worked with Odin Teatret from 1973 to 1974. He took part in the group performances *The Book of Dances* and *Johann Sebastian Bach*.

4 The transmission of experience

I was told that everything began in Oslo in 1964 with five young people between the ages of nineteen and twenty (each of whom had attempted and failed to enter the Statens Teater Skole of Oslo) and a young director, Eugenio Barba, who wanted to create his own theatre group and who began to transmit to them the physical and vocal training that he had seen in the theatre of Jerzy Grotowski.[1]

Each of these five young people could do something which the others did not know how to do: ballet, gymnastics or pantomime. Every day, after the work led by Eugenio, they took it in turns to lead sessions and exchange their abilities. In this way they learnt to transmit their individual experience.

They prepared scenes or little *études* from the very first day of work, and after a brief period they also began to rehearse their first performance, *Ornitofilene*, based on a text by a contemporary Norwegian writer, Jens Bjørnboe.[2]

A few days before the premiere, one of the five actors left the group. The performance had to be reworked before it toured Scandinavia. In 1966, after a performance in Viborg (Denmark), Odin Teatret received an offer of board and lodging from the Danish town of Holstebro which wanted to change its commercial image to that of a centre of cultural life.[3] Eugenio Barba and his actors, who had no prospects of subsidies in Norway, accepted the offer. When the moment of relocation arrived, three actors emigrated with Barba to Denmark, including Else Marie Laukvik (who is still active in the group) and Torgeir Wethal (who was active in the group until his death in 2010).

With the ensemble reduced, it was no longer possible to keep performing *Ornitofilene*. Odin Teatret needed to recruit new performers at once, and this happened by means of workshops in which participants could experience working under the direction of Eugenio Barba. Torgeir taught acrobatics and Else Marie composition, about which I will speak later. Iben Nagel Rasmussen joined the group in this period.

At the same time Eugenio Barba also began to organise workshops aimed at Scandinavian scholars, inviting big names from the contemporary theatre scene. Over the years, these pedagogical situations have changed name and structure – International Seminar, ISTA (International School of Theatre Anthropology), Odin Week – but they still continue to form part of Odin Teatret's artistic and economic strategy.

During the first twelve years of the group's life the basics of training were taught by Eugenio Barba and the more experienced actors (the 'senior ones') – that is, Torgeir, Else Marie and Iben. They transmitted their practical experience to me, but Eugenio Barba was my master. I was the last Odin Teatret actress to be educated under his direct guidance.

From 1976 onwards Eugenio started to maintain that he already had all the actors he needed, and he decided that from that moment the only possibility of joining the group was to be 'adopted' by one of the performers who would be responsible both for the education and the upkeep of the student. So it happened that Tage adopted Francis Pardeilhan[4] and Julia Varley,[5] and Iben adopted Toni Cots[6] and Silvia Ricciardelli.[7] With the exception of Richard Fowler,[8] Toni Cots, and Tina Nielsen,[9] who had already graduated from a theatre school, all the performers of Odin Teatret, from the beginning until today, have been educated within the group.

In the autumn of 1974, after only six months with the group, Eugenio Barba asked me to lead the training with objects for the ten participants of the International Brigade.[10] This task was of utmost importance in my formation. In order to be able to transmit my experience in a clear and efficient way, I was obliged to formulate it first for myself. Teaching allowed me to take possession of my knowledge. This understanding was to accompany me throughout the course of my professional life.

During our tours with *The Book of Dances* and *Come! And the Day Will be Ours*, Eugenio invited me to assist the clown workshops conducted by Jan Torp for other theatre groups and drama schools.

When I began to lead workshops on my own, I committed myself to transmitting the training that I had learned from my companions. I would spend a lot of time teaching students how to do a headstand or a shoulder stand, without knowing how to link these exercises in a context that justified their existence in the actor's training. I took it for granted that, having chosen to do a workshop with an Odin Teatret

The ensemble of *Brecht's Ashes* and *The Million* (1978). Top left: Torgeir Wethal, Tage Larsen, Leif Beck, Eugenio Barba, Torben Bjelke, Tom Fjordefalk, Francis Pardeilhan, Toni Cots and Else Marie Laukvik. Bottom left: Silvia Ricciardelli, Julia Varley, Iben Nagel Rasmussen and Roberta Carreri.

actress, the participants knew what the training served. On the other hand, I would not have been able to explain it clearly to them. At the time, training for me was a daily challenge by which I gauged the strength of my will and determination to form part of the group – a kind of Sun Dance that lasted for months.[11]

During my first two years as a pedagogue, my greatest fear was of meeting someone among the students who could do the work I taught better than me – so I strove to make the exercises extremely difficult.

Several years later, in 1988, I conducted a three-month workshop with six students, entitled 'Winter Seeds'. From that moment I began to identify a nucleus of principles as a starting point that would allow me to transmit, in a brief time, what for me was essential in training:

- how to find one's own scenic presence;
- how to acquire a formalised scenic behaviour free from the automatisms of everyday life;
- how to free oneself from one's own professional automatisms, one's own clichés.

By the end of the 1990s I had managed to distil a pedagogical structure for my workshops that I called 'The Dance of Intentions' and which consists of:

- perceiving one's own presence in relation to the space and the other actors;
- being in the action that one is performing and at the same time open to what is happening around oneself, ready to react;
- finding the central axis of the body and working with what I call 'the snake', that 'invisible muscle' which runs along the spinal column from the eyes to the coccyx and which is the seat of *in-tensions* (I will explain the concept of *in-tensions*, which is so important in my work as an actress and a pedagogue, later on);
- how to reach dynamic immobility;
- exploring different qualities of focus in the eyes;
- identifying different points in the body where the leading impulse of a movement in space can start;
- the creation of physical and vocal actions, and how to perform them with different qualities of energy;
- work on slow motion;
- vocal training with multiple body resonators;
- the relation between vocal and physical actions.

Looking back at the professional path I followed, I now recognise how the tradition of the transmission of experience at Odin Teatret was an answer to a real and specific pedagogical need that has developed over the years and which has manifested itself in various ways.

In addition to seeing our performances, anyone interested in the work of our group has the possibility of knowing more about us by reading books and articles written on Odin Teatret or by its members, seeing films and videos of performances and work demonstrations or documentation of pedagogical situations such as ISTA, attending work demonstrations, and doing workshops with Odin Teatret members.

In the first work demonstration of Odin Teatret, *Moon and Darkness*, presented in the 1980s, Iben Nagel Rasmussen went through the various stages of her training and showed how she had composed some of her characters.

Over the years other Odin Teatret performers who had developed and personalised their training turned to work demonstrations as a means of communication that, on the one hand, has all the technical information and practical examples of a workshop and, on the other, retains the dramaturgy and scenic presence of the actor in a performance.

In 1988 I was invited to present the performance *Judith* at the Teatro Stabile of L'Aquila.[12] On that occasion Nando Taviani asked me to hold a daily three-hour encounter with his university students.

Assisted by Torgeir Wethal's films on the training and performances of Odin Teatret, I narrated my professional history from the very first steps under the guidance of Eugenio Barba and the more expert actors, up to the creation of *Judith*. Even deducting the time it took to screen the films, there emerged an artistic biography of six hours' duration. At the end of these encounters, which lasted for three days, Nando Taviani suggested that I turn that biography into a work demonstration. Back in Holstebro I condensed the narrative, and after a little time *Traces in the Snow* took shape. Eugenio worked on my concrete proposal, making a few very important changes without altering its structure.

The form of my work demonstration is set, but it is not rigid. Every now and again I may highlight some specific aspects of our work or introduce new themes that I consider relevant at the moment or in a given situation. To do this, however, I am compelled to remove other parts to retain its duration within acceptable limits.

Notes

1 This refers to the Theatre of 13 Rows (Teatr 13 Rzedów) of Opole, which from 1959 onwards was under the direction of Jerzy Grotowski and Ludwik Flaszen, and was where Eugenio Barba served his apprenticeship between 1961 and 1964. In autumn 1962 Grotowski's theatre adopted the name 'Theatre Laboratory of 13 Rows'. In 1967, after more than a year based in Wrocław, the theatre became known as the 'Theatre Laboratory (Institute of the Research of the Actor's Method)'. Information on Barba's period in Poland can be found in two books written by him: *Alla Ricerca del Teatro Perduto* (In Search of a Lost Theatre, Padova: Marsilio, 1965), and *Land of Ashes and Diamonds: My Apprenticeship in Poland, followed by 26 Letters from Jerzy Grotowski to Eugenio Barba* (Aberystwyth: Black Mountain Press, 1999).
2 *Ornitofilene* (The Bird-Lovers), 1965–66. Actors: Anne-Trine Grimnes, Else Marie Laukvik, Tor Sannum and Torgeir Wethal. Text by Jens Bjørnboe. Adaptation and direction: Eugenio Barba.
3 The distinctive cultural policy of Holstebro is tackled by Ingvar Holm, Viveka Hagnell, and Jane Rasch, in *A Model for Culture Holstebro* (Stockholm: Almquist & Wiksell International, 1985 [originally published in Danish in 1977]).
4 Francis Pardeilhan, an American actor of Odin Teatret from 1976 to 1987. He took part in the group performances *Johann Sebastian Bach, Anabasis, The Million, Brecht's Ashes,* and *The Gospel According to Oxyrhincus.*

5 Julia Varley is an English actress who joined Odin Teatret in 1976. Since then she has taken part in all the group performances and in the solos *The Castle of Holstebro* (1990–current, dramaturgy and direction by Eugenio Barba) and *Doña Musica's Butterflies* (1997–current, dramaturgy and direction by Eugenio Barba). Since its foundation in 1986, she has also formed part of The Magdalena Project: International Network of Women in Contemporary Theatre. In 1992 she founded Transit, an international theatre festival under her artistic direction and hosted by Odin Teatret. In addition she is the editor of the theatre journal *The Open Page*.

6 Toni Cots, a Spanish actor of Odin Teatret from 1977 to 1984. He took part in the group performances *Johann Sebastian Bach*, *The Million*, *Anabasis*, *Brecht's Ashes*, and the solo *The Story of Oedipus*.

7 Silvia Ricciardelli, an Italian actress of Odin Teatret from 1976 to 1984. She took part in the group performances *Johann Sebastian Bach*, *The Million*, *Anabasis*, and *Brecht's Ashes*.

8 Richard Fowler, a Canadian actor of Odin Teatret from 1987 to 1989. He took part in the group performances *Talabot* and *Rooms in the Emperor's Palace*.

9 Tina Nielsen, a Danish actress of Odin Teatret from 1992 to 1997. She took part in the group performances *Rooms in the Emperor's Palace* and *Kaosmos*.

10 The first (1974–75) and second (1975–76) International Brigades were six-month workshops held at Odin Teatret. The participants of the first Brigade paid for the workshop by building a prefabricated annex in the back garden of Odin Teatret.

11 An initiation rite performed on the occasion of the summer solstice by various native North American tribes, symbolising, by means of a cycle of deaths and rebirths, a process of regeneration.

12 *Judith*, 1987–present. Actress: Roberta Carreri. Dramaturgy and direction: Eugenio Barba.

5 Exercises and principles

Reflecting upon the story of my training, I realise that since joining Odin Teatret in 1974, it has gone through four seasons.

I call them seasons because there is no clear demarcation line separating one period from another. Just as one can perceive the first signs of autumn during a day in August, so in a training phase one can identify the embryo of a new principle: the result of a need that in time will bring us to further development. Even their duration is not the same: some can last two years, others more than ten.

Today I am able to recognise how the aim of the first season was to discover new ways of 'thinking the body' and find my scenic presence through exercises taught to me by others.

In the second season I began to develop an individual training, incorporating principles I created. At this time I also began to utilise the training to break those clichés that had consolidated themselves in my work over the years.

In the third season, training became the space wherein I concentrated on the organisation of physical scores – that is, on fixed sequences of actions. I developed scenes and dances with the assistance of music and objects.

Now, in the fourth season, I am moved by a kind of existential necessity that concretises itself in a theme. From this starting point I search for texts, music, objects, clothes, light and elements of scenography to create sequences of actions and dances, to construct a montage that has dramaturgical coherence.

I have worked with both exercises and principles in training.

Exercises have a fixed structure that allows their transmission: a beginning, a development and an end. For example, acrobatic exercises as well as 'physical exercises',[1] such as the plastique ones which the Odin Teatret performers learnt directly from Ryszard

Cieślak in the 1960s[2] or the 'Swiss exercises' based on falls and ways of sitting down and standing up which Iben developed in her training in the early 1970s, have a fixed structure.

On the other hand, work on a principle involves a frame of rules within which one can act.

Acrobatic exercises were fundamental in the formation of all Odin Teatret actors. In the process of learning them, the body and mind must be one: if one thinks of other matters while performing an acrobatic exercise, it is highly probable that one will fall and hurt oneself. That is why I like to say that the floor has been my first Zen master: it awoke me each and every time I lost my concentration.

At Odin Teatret, learning occurred by means of imitation. Torgeir led the collective sessions on acrobatics for the first twelve years; I participated in the final two years of this period. He would execute a gymnastic exercise on a training mat in the middle of the space, and straight away we would try to do exactly the same, repeating it two or three times. Torgeir would then show it again, indicating on his body the points we were getting wrong. Teaching occurred in silence. Words were used only rarely in the process. We had to observe attentively: half of the work consisted in learning to 'read' the essential point of the exercise in the teacher's body.

The sustained rhythm with which we worked was aimed at overcoming mental blocks, and thus also physical ones, caused by fear. Once a series of exercises was learnt, we moved on to improvising their sequence and executing them using different dynamics. When we felt secure enough we would do them on the wooden floor without the protection of the mat, thus moving in various directions in the space. The fact that there were several people on the floor led us to be careful and to react to the sudden appearance of a colleague in front of us, changing direction at the last instant. Collisions could be painful. This controlled risk was, for me, an essential element of one aspect of training.

One word which Eugenio used and still uses repeatedly during the work is *sats*, which is the Norwegian word for 'impulse'.

I can also define *sats* as the intention to accomplish a precise action. In the moment I accumulate the necessary mental energies, which are consequently also physical, to execute a one-metre-long leap, I enter a position of *sats*. I am not in *sats* position if my legs are fully extended. To be in *sats* position allows me to react and change direction at any moment. It allows me to be unpredictable. Being in *sats* position implies being present in the moment.

The precision of *sats* and the rapidity of reflexes were indispensable conditions in acrobatics, as well as in the exercise with the plastic stick (where you had to dodge a colleague's hit by either jumping or lowering your head), and in the one where you had to run and jump to touch precisely the sternum of a colleague with the tip of your feet. These exercises were aimed at familiarising us with being precise with our *sats* and our eyes, so that our colleagues could react accurately. The objective was not to mislead them, but to give them, quickly, clear information to which they could reply rapidly.

The first years of my training included walks and positions for which the basic principles were taught by Iben. One of them was called the 'samurai'. The presence of samurai, like that of swordsmen, is characterised by the fact that every one of their movements is full of that *extra-ordinary* presence typical of moments of risk. They are alert. They are present. They are in *sats* position. But they can react correctly only if they are not blocked by fear.

Thanks to training it is possible to acquire a motor ability and a physical memory that enhances one's self-confidence. Once the mind-body unity is achieved, one should concentrate only on inhabiting the moment, keeping the mind, the eyes and the ears open, ready to react.

One should not confuse this kind of presence with tension. A cat, a skier, a bull-fighter are able to react at any moment because they are not tense: their knowledge is embodied.

Notes

1   'Physical exercises' are clearly identifiable by means of precise names such as the *bridge*, the *dwarf bridge*, and the *candle*.
2   Ryszard Cieślak was an actor of Jerzy Grotowski's Laboratory Theatre. In July 1966, together with Grotowski and Stanislaw Brzozowski, Cieślak conducted a fifteen-day workshop on physical training: it was the first initiative organised by Odin Teatret in Holstebro, inaugurating the tradition of 'inter-Scandinavian workshops' which lasted until 1977 and which brought to Denmark many masters of Western and Asian traditions of theatre and dance. Cieślak, together with Grotowski and other pedagogues, held two other workshops in Holstebro in 1967 and 1968. The film *Training at Grotowski's* Teatr-Laboratorium *in Wrocław* (directed by Torgeir Wethal and produced by Odin Teatret Film in 1972) is an important document that shows Cieślak's work as a pedagogue and the basics of his physical training (the film documents a work session with two Odin Teatret performers, Malou Illmoni and Tage Larsen). For another account of the workshops held by Cieślak and Grotowski in Holstebro, see Eugenio Barba, *Land of Ashes and Diamonds: My Apprenticeship in Poland, followed by 26 Letters from Jerzy Grotowski to Eugenio Barba* (Aberystwyth: Black Mountain Press, 1999). Ryszard Cieślak died in 1990.

6   Slow motion

Apart from acrobatics, Torgeir also taught the principles of the work on balance and slow motion. For the former, he made us jump forward and land on the sole of one foot, and we had to keep our balance in that position until the moment we decided to jump in another direction. He suggested that we do this by looking at a point on the wall in front of us. 'Cling to the point with your eyes!'

To teach us how to move in slow motion, Torgeir asked us to take enormous steps that challenged our balance. Again, in order not to fall, we had to fix our eyes on a precise spot on the wall in front of us. In this way the nape of my neck and my foot on the floor became the extreme points of a curve along which I had to create oppositions that varied from moment to moment in order to keep my balance while moving.

Torgeir used to tell us that it was important to avoid the daily position of entropic equilibrium (with the centre of gravity placed exactly between parallel legs), and to explore positions of extreme balance that required all of our physical intelligence. Learning how to perform some physical exercises in slow motion – such as handstands, headstands, bridges and somersaults – was essential for the development of my physical intelligence.

To take a big step forward in slow motion, I begin by lifting my right leg behind me while my torso stretches forward; then, rotating on the pivot of my left leg and with my pelvis as a fulcrum, I draw an arch a metre off the ground with my right leg. At the same time, my torso moves to the left until it leans backwards and my right leg finds itself in front of me. Slowly, I lower my foot to the ground while still keeping all the weight on my left leg. It is only at this point that I shift my weight onto my right foot and either complete the step or lift my foot again to move in another direction.

Moving with extreme slowness is not part of our daily technique. So I have to think constantly with every part of my body to avoid involuntarily speeding up any movements.

If acrobatics helps me to overcome the barrier of fear by restricting the time for reflection, slow motion helps me to visualise mentally every detail of the moving body. Working with the force of gravity, I push or hold the weight of my body, centimetre by centimetre, moving in the space.

I imagine the blood running slowly in my veins and my breath becoming fuller.

The plait of my hair falls on the ground while I am doing a somersault in slow motion because I cannot dominate it. But I should be able to control the rest of my body: hands, feet, arms, legs, torso, head ... I also have to think of all the parts of my body simultaneously to be able to prevent problems that may emerge later on. For example, if I do not move my right hand forward when I am beginning a somersault, it will not arrive in time to touch the floor and prevent my weight from falling in that direction.

I cannot speed up any gesture. So, before reaching the floor with my feet, I have to think of the right way to place them in order to stand up again without any abrupt movements. By leaning forward I lift up my bottom from the floor, thus freeing a leg from my weight and allowing me to stand up on my feet very slowly. To keep my arms from moving too rapidly, I have to do the action of pushing the air with my arms and hands, imagining that it is offering resistance, as if I am moving in a sea of molasses.

If I want to sit down, I have to create an internal resistance that keeps me from falling at the last moment. The body is going down, but the mind is thinking up. A one-centimetre fall is still a fall. In this state of *continuous sats* I can freeze the action at any moment.

Slow motion does not simply consist of 'moving slowly'; it is also the result of an internal impulse that starts from the 'snake'. I define the eyes as the first vertebra or the head of the 'snake' and the coccyx as its tail.

The work on a principle offers a frame of rules within which variations can be performed. I can thus improvise with the principle of slow motion without performing fixed exercises, but I have to keep a constant eye on not breaking the basic rule of moving very slowly. I can, for example, move in slow motion by means of oppositions, indicating various directions in the space with various parts of the body: I look to the left, move my right elbow backwards, shift my pelvis to the right indicating in front of me with my left hand, change the direction of my eyes, of my left arm, and of my right arm, I lower myself, step to the right.

A forward roll in slow motion.

In this way I create a body from which, like a Cubist statue, various vectors of energies are radiated simultaneously and in various directions in the space. The important thing is to abide by the rule of moving slowly.

If I lose balance my movements accelerate, thus violating the rule that defines the principle within which I am working. So I have to go back and repeat the step in a correct manner.

7 Composition

Another principle that formed part of the first season of my training was composition with legs and feet, arms and hands.

The aim of this work is to liberate the actor from the automatisms of everyday life, those which follow the rule of maximum result with minimum effort. If I have to go from A to B, I take the shortest route:

Examples of composition with the feet. Left: pushing waves. Right: walking on a slab of marble under a burning sun.

a straight line. The opposite rule applies in training. If I have to go from A to B, I begin by proceeding in the opposite direction. In this way I create a counter-impulse and a change in direction, and I move along curved or serrated lines. I create moments of surprise, unexpected reversals, before I reach my destination. Dancing with my *sats* in this way, I accustom myself not to anticipate actions.

As newborn babies we explore the various possibilities of our hands and feet, but the moment we learn to walk we adopt a functional modality of using the body. In the course of time, we have become so able and proficient that we can walk without having to think about it. Walking has become part of our body's everyday technique and as such it is now an automatism.

The aim of the composition work with legs and feet is to try out new possibilities of moving the body by means of mental images capable of

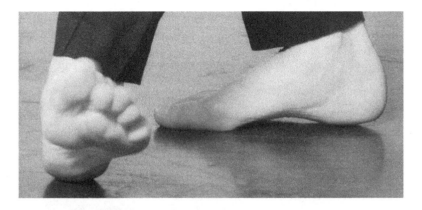

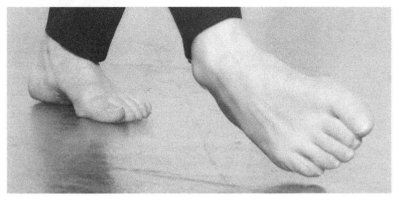

Examples of composition with the feet. Top: like a boat riding the waves. Bottom: like a plough in a field.

reawakening physical associations. For example, caressing the floor with the feet; moving like a plough in a field; walking on a slab of marble under a burning sun; marching like a Russian soldier; using the tip of the foot like a dog sniffing a trail; walking on tiptoes like Sylvester the Cat; retreating from and kicking waves in front of me; shifting sand sideways; walking as if the feet were snakes; making big steps like a samurai.

I can work in the same principle with arms and hands. The hands that we use all the time but which we rarely dance with can become, for example, butterflies that play on an abyss; waves on a faraway sea; fireworks; arrows that I cast from my chest; crabs ready for battle; a shining tiara on my head; the opening petals of a flower; fish that dart in a pond; leaves falling from trees; a melting snowman; a weeping willow in the wind.

Working with this principle, my attention is directed at the hands or the feet. But these are not the only parts that move: all the body is engaged when I work with the principle of composition. I change

Examples of composition with the hands. Left: a shining tiara on my head. Right: butterflies that play on an abyss.

Composition 35

Example of composition with the hands: leaves falling from trees.

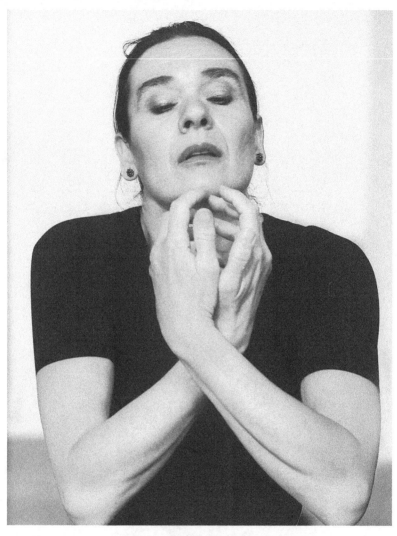

Example of composition with the hands: the opening petals of a flower.

direction and speed with every image, trying to avoid those pauses that are characteristic of the division between thought and action.

This principle provides the actor with the possibility of finding a way of being natural on stage without appearing naturalistic. The rich possibilities that present themselves during composition help to enhance the actor's self-confidence and the capacity to react promptly and in a pertinent way to the director's requests.

8 Introversion and extroversion

The principle of introversion and extroversion was also transmitted to me by the more senior colleagues during the first season of my training.

Its point of departure consists of the fact that I can 'introvert' or 'extrovert' every part of my body. We can also use the words 'closed' or 'open'. For example: the head can bend downwards (introverted) or upwards (extroverted); the shoulders can flex forward (introverted) or backward (extroverted); the pelvis rotates forward (introverted) or backward (extroverted); the arms can fold around the torso (introverted) or be open wide (extroverted); the hands can be closed (introverted) or open (extroverted); the legs can have the knees turned inward (introverted) or outward (extroverted); the feet follow the legs.

Working with this principle I create a dialogue between the various parts of my body. For example: head introverted; shoulders introverted; arms extroverted; one hand introverted and one hand extroverted; pelvis extroverted; one leg extroverted and the other introverted. Hands extroverted while the arms are introverted, or the opposite.

I can be completely extroverted and change only one detail: the head.

Sometimes, certain positions are created during this dialogue between the various parts of the body that awake in me precise images which reappear again during the daily training and which in time develop into fixed forms. Even if all this belongs to the natural development of the training within a principle, I have to continue the research on new combinations and not repeat only those forms which are known to me.

This principle, like the previous ones, obliges me not only to think with the body but also to consider my relationship with the space

Examples of dialogue between the various parts of my body, introverted and extroverted respectively.

Introversion and extroversion

within which I move. To make it live I change direction frequently, I move along straight or curved lines, in circles or diagonals, parallel with or perpendicular to the lines that delineate the space in which I am working.

I am a statue that undergoes various metamorphoses, while moving and conquering new positions in the space.

9 Denmark

During the winter in Denmark, seven in the morning is still the dead of night.

When I arrived in Holstebro in October 1974, Iben and Torgeir proposed that I stay in their house even though it had already been put up for sale. After two months we had to leave, and we relocated to the countryside. Some months later I moved again so that I could live on my own in the annex behind the theatre which the first International Brigade had just built.

During my first two years with Odin Teatret I moved house six times. Relocating was not a huge problem. My few possessions could fit in a suitcase and in four wooden crates branded with the word 'Carlsberg'. In the past the crates had served to transport beer bottles; now I used them as a library, a bedside table and a chest of drawers.

In the autumn of 1975 Tom Fjordefalk[1] and I rented a small house at the edge of a wood with two rooms and a kitchen, which other Odin Teatret actors had inhabited in the past. The house did not have any running water so we had to draw water from a pump in the garden – and in winter the water froze. We had one bicycle between the two of us. While Tom pedalled and panted for the five kilometres that separated us from the theatre, I sat on the luggage rack and froze. After our first tour in South America in 1976 we bought a very old car. Two months later I went back to live in the theatre, this time in a room in the attic.

In the mid-1970s Odin Teatret was situated on the periphery of a rapidly growing city. It served as a link between a neighbourhood of detached houses, fenced in by privet hedges and uncultivated fields, where we went running in the morning.

Running on the beaches of Salento was a completely different experience to doing so on the frost-covered fields of Denmark. Here the moon is still high up in the sky and the stars still twinkle in those

Odin Teatret in the late 1960s.

winter mornings when it does not rain. I had read that in his first years with Odin Teatret, Ulrik thought about the beard of Karl Marx to cope with the hard training. Running with freezing snot under my nose I thought of Ulrik thinking about the beard of Karl Marx.

Running was followed by an hour of acrobatics. Starting the day in this way literally made me throw up. After the first two days I started to have breakfast during the mid-morning break.

When I lived on my own in the little room of the annex behind the theatre, I got to know the great Scandinavian silence for the first time, the same silence which permeated the films of Ingmar Bergman that I had seen in the art house cinemas in Milan. This overwhelming silence that made my ears hum seemed to be literally tangible. It was anguishing. In Italy the noise of everyday life throbbed around me and poured into my mind. Here, in silence, I could hear my thoughts more clearly.

Denmark was an abstract entity for me during my first years with Odin Teatret. I worked all day long in the theatre, and with the exception of the supermarket, the library, the dentist, the doctor and the bank, my contact with Holstebro was for all intents and purposes non-existent. I lived on 'planet Odin', and not having any friends or family in Denmark, I had no idea about the land in which I was living. Deprived of the possibility of communicating in my own language, I found solace in diaries.

Odin Teatret in 2006.

I think that one of the first pieces of advice that Eugenio gave me in Carpignano was to keep a work diary. Diaries (private and work-related) became my confidantes and my memory. At school I had learnt how to take notes, but now, having to transcribe sequences of actions and dances, I invented a new annotation system.

On my arrival in Carpignano, Eugenio had asked Elsa Kvamme to teach me Norwegian.[2] This was the Scandinavian language spoken by Eugenio, Torgeir, Elsa herself and Else Marie. Tom was Swedish.

Due to the intense rhythm of the work and the tours I never had the opportunity to learn Danish at school. I had a very imprecise idea of the language because the way in which the words are pronounced made it impossible for me to imagine their spelling. That is why it was very difficult for me to learn it by ear.

In 1976 Francis Pardeilhan entered the group and my private life. At first we spoke French amongst ourselves, but later we used English. Our daughter Alice, born in 1981, grew up speaking three languages at the same time: Italian, English and Danish. In fact it was Alice who brought me in contact with the town of Holstebro. The world that revolved around her – *dagmamma*,[3] primary school, the after-school activity centre, music school, horse-riding, and secondary school – brought me into contact with a part of the town's population that I would not have otherwise met. To communicate with Alice's schoolmates and friends I had to learn Danish at last.

I can say that it was Alice who brought me to Denmark.

Notes

1 Tom Fjordefalk, a Swedish actor of Odin Teatret from 1974 to 1984. He took part in the group performances *The Book of Dances, Come! And the Day Will Be Ours, Anabasis,* and *The Million.*
2 Elsa Kvamme, a Norwegian actress of Odin Teatret from 1973 to 1975. She took part in the group performance *The Book of Dances.*
3 *Dagmamma* means 'day mother' in Danish. In Denmark it is possible to set up a small private nursery for five children run by a *dagmamma* if a house, which is inhabited by a family, has certain characteristics established by the municipality. The persons who make use of the nursery pay a monthly fee to the municipality which in turn pays the *dagmamma* a fixed salary.

10 Geronimo and street theatre

Geronimo, my character in *Anabasis*, was born in July 1976.[1]

I was on Moen, a small Danish island, with Jan Torp and Silvia Ricciardelli, the latter having just participated in the second six-month workshop of the International Brigade. We had been invited to present street theatre interventions within the framework of an international festival.

Since I had arrived directly from our holidays, I did not have a costume with me – I only had a top hat which I had bought in a second-hand shop. Jan, who was one metre ninety tall and weighed ninety kilos, lent me shoes, dinner jacket trousers, a white shirt and a necktie. Everything was clean and in good condition, but everything was too big for me.

A pair of red shoulder straps resolved the width issue of the trousers. I also needed to shorten the trousers to remedy their excessive length, but I went a little too far in my endeavours and my ankles ended up exposed and vulnerable, sprouting from a pair of size forty-four shoes.

I was tanned and had a bob hairstyle. A Yanomami in the heart of the Amazon forest had cut my hair like that in April during our tour in Venezuela with *Come! And the Day Will be Ours*.

When I looked in the mirror I was reminded of one of those oddly funny daguerreotype North American Indians who dressed up in elegant European clothes before being photographed. I baptised myself Geronimo in honour of the great Apache chief. Geronimo was born from a costume and from the nostalgia for absolute innocence.

It was summer and Geronimo held a straw in his mouth as he clung to Jan's hand and looked at the world with wide open and dreamy eyes. His breath was as slow as his movements, which were light and wavering. He moved in the streets to the sound of Silvia's accordion. Silvia wore a black dinner jacket and a red curly wig reminiscent of

Harpo Marx. Looking people in the eye, Geronimo managed to overcome the distance that separates two strangers. He slowly stretched out his hands towards an ice-cream and took it from an astonished child. But Jan intervened before the child had time to cry, ordering Geronimo to return the ice-cream immediately. I rediscovered the world in Jan's shadow, looking around me through the naive eyes of Geronimo.

The creation of this simple-spirited male character freed me from a series of feminine behavioural clichés that had ingrained themselves in my work.

During the week that we stayed on Moen, Geronimo had the possibility of consolidating himself as a character. It was there that Francis Pardeilhan, who was participating in the festival as an actor with the British company Ladies and Gentlemen, became interested in me and our work.

Initially Geronimo was mute, but after a couple of months Jan discovered bird whistles: a duck for him and a raven for me. In this way we emerged from our silence.

Geronimo with Jan Torp (Volterra, 1976).

I felt a huge sorrow in 1978 when Jan communicated his intention to leave Odin Teatret. Geronimo would lose his support, the big brother who protected him from the world and sorted things out after his pranks.

Now on his own, Geronimo had to develop other characteristics. So he took on a livelier and more dance-like dynamic. His hat, shoes and 'voice' (the duck whistle that had been Jan's) are his mask.

Geronimo has shaken hands with people from all over the world and of every social class. If his voice frightens dogs or children, Geronimo is in turn alarmed and escapes or retreats timidly.

Geronimo is one of my keys to the world. There is only one thing that terrifies him: getting on a tightrope stretched high up between two houses.

In September 1976, Odin Teatret and Bread and Puppet Theatre held a big itinerant performance along the main street of Pontedera.[2] Francis Pardeilhan had just arrived in Italy and was holding one end of the rope behind the window from which I emerged. Knud Erik Knudsen, our technician, held the other end from a window in the opposite building. Jan and I were balancing in mid-air: two clowns on a rope. No one thought that my fall was an accident: I landed directly on my backside in front of the 'pink piglet' mask of Torgeir's Dwarf, who promptly gathered the companions with a whistle. The parade proceeded as usual with Geronimo in the rear. His rather odd walk seemed to be part of his character.

At the time I hardly felt the pain thanks to the adrenaline generated in situations of performance (and of danger). It was a different story a few hours later when an enormous bruise appeared.

Exactly two years later, in Aarhus, a tightrope was stretched over a pedestrian street. One end of the rope disappeared in one of those windows that are blocked from the inside and which can only be opened halfway. This was not important because I had to get off the rope by sitting on the shoulders of Tage, who was on stilts. I had ventured out onto the rope by clinging to it with my hands and crossing my ankles around it. Having reached the midpoint, I slowly lowered myself down while still clinging to the rope with my hands. On stilts and with outstretched arms, Tage could only barely touch my feet. I looked at the window where the rope disappeared. I felt my strength ebbing away. There was only one way out. My hands let go of the rope before I had time to be afraid. Tage seized my feet in mid-air, but they slipped through his fingers. Seeing the blue sky under my feet I thought: 'You should never grab the feet of someone who's falling because that way she'll fall on her head.'

Geronimo and Jan on a tightrope (Pontedera, 1976).

I did not feel the blow. Suddenly it became dark.

Around me, silence. Blood on the pavement. I still have the shattered top hat as a testimony to my fall. Some say it saved my life.

My spine, however, was irretrievably damaged. When I was operated on in 1992 for a cervical disc hernia that had paralysed my left arm, they found that the disc between the fourth and fifth cervical vertebrae had been broken for fourteen years. The operation involved welding the two vertebrae, in the process reducing the mobility of the nape.

Geronimo's fall led to a change in my training, but I continued to work and travel.

Travelling makes me anxious and my pain threshold is very low. If I have done this work for many years it is not because I am a martyr or a masochist. I have remained with Odin Teatret because I was able to listen to something deep within me that made me understand the need for it. Our way of life, full of travels and creatively stimulating challenges, can fascinate many people, but one needs a profound motivation to go along with it.

Geronimo was in Africa, in the Upper Volta (today Burkina Faso), in June 1982.[3] For the first time ever he was on his own. Out of habit, I kept a diary of that journey. Here are some fragments.

50   *The story and the training*

Geronimo in Peru (1978).

Dori, Upper Volta, June 1982
   Up to now it has been easy to identify me: a griotte *(their name for jesters) who dances with other* griots. *Today I will leave the scenic space and move around the domain of ordinary people.*
   The market is five minutes to the left of our house.
   The peak period is between ten in the morning and noon. Today, for the first time, Geronimo will walk the street on his own, without the protection of his Odin Teatret companions.
   Geronimo leaves the house, walking slowly. As soon as he enters the market zone he notices that the women are afraid. They see a white woman, dressed as a man, with a bizarre hat on her head, with shoes too big for her,

and a strange black thing in her mouth that produces a rather irreverent sound. They surely think that I am crazy. Only mad people walk around the streets making fools of themselves. But as Geronimo skips along, the children look him in the eye and laugh.

Somehow this reassures the women, who, looking at each other, seem to be saying: if she amuses the children, then she cannot be dangerous.

A crowd of yelling children begins to follow me around. There is the risk that one of them might knock over the gourd calebasse containers lying on the ground filled with fruit and seeds. So, once in the market, I make sure that I choose the widest passages or walk slowly in the narrow ones. In the few open spaces that I find, I do an about-turn and rapidly fling myself upon my pursuers who flee laughing away, but who then follow me again the moment I turn my back. They shout a word at me which I do not manage to decipher. It seems like they are saying Salò. Salaud? ('Bastard' in French.) I couldn't believe it.

I remember that in Ayacucho, in the Peruvian Andes, a little boy who followed us in the local market had said that Geronimo was the Devil because his feet were too long.

Now, an old man dressed in indigo looks sternly at me, shakes his head as a rebuff, stretches an arm, and points a thin index finger in the faraway distance. I stop, I look at his arm, at his eyes, and at his finger ... and then run squawking in that direction followed by a crowd of shouting children. At the first corner I turn to the left and walk into the tailors' big white patio where I make a triumphal entrance, dragging behind me my cackling retinue who, out of a sense of occasion, begin to imitate my gait.

After exiting the tailors' patio, I walk around the market and arrive in front of our Land Rover. I take refuge inside it while the little children assault the vehicle. Through the glass, my eyes meet those of the child who had followed me very closely most of the time and who had been among the first to articulate that word. I just about opened the window to ask him: 'But what do you keep shouting?'

'Sarlot.'

'What does it mean?'

'It is the name of a little white man with a black hat on his head and with long feet like yours, who walks with a little boy by his side.'

'Where have you seen him?'

'At the cinema of the missions.'

The film they had seen was Charlie Chaplin's The Kid.

It was the first time in my life that I had been mistaken for Charlot.

The following day we repeat the action in the market in order to film it. The camera operator, the sound technician and Mette leave the house before me. To film my entrance in the market they had to assemble the camera on the roof of the Land Rover.

Alone, in the deserted house, I tie my bow tie in front of a mirror. I feel like an exotic animal, a circus freak. I'm afraid.

This time the children will assault me the moment I appear, the adults will hate me for the damage the children will cause in the market, and at the end I will have to seek refuge again in the Land Rover.

I say to myself: the important thing is not to be afraid. If I am not afraid, my eyes will be transparent and the people will not be aggressive. Everything will be fine. The important thing is that the children do not touch me. If they touch Geronimo it's over.

It's time to go.

From the doorstep of the house I can see the camera operator on the Land Rover's roof in the corner of the market.

I walk slowly, greeting my neighbours.

Just before I arrive at the market I meet the Haussa man who had been dancing with knives at my first barter in Dori. We shake hands. He looks at my shoes. I tell him that I am dressed like this because I am on my way to the market to work.

'To dance?'

'More or less.'

As soon as I take my leave from him, I put the whistle in my mouth, turn suddenly and meet the eyes of a boy. He smiles. Geronimo has begun. There is no longer a reason to be afraid.

Today even the women laugh.

Notes

1 *Anabasis*, 1977–84. An itinerant performance. Actors: Torben Bjelke, Roberta Carreri, Toni Cots, Tom Fjordefalk, Tage Larsen, Else Marie Laukvik, Francis Pardeilhan, Iben Nagel Rasmussen, Silvia Ricciardelli, Gustavo Riondet, Ulrik Skeel, Julia Varley and Torgeir Wethal (some of the actors participated in only one of the various versions). Direction: Eugenio Barba.
2 Bread and Puppet Theatre was founded by Peter Schumann in New York in 1961.
3 The journey is documented in *Dances in the Sand*, a film produced and directed by Danish anthropologist Mette Bovin in 1983. The film tackles a cultural barter within the context of 'provocation anthropology'. The film portrays the participation of an actress, an anthropologist and the inhabitants of an African village in an exchange of dances, theatre, songs, 'hyena dance', masks and drum rhythms. See Matte Bovin, 'Provocation Anthropology: Bartering Performance in Africa', in Ian Watson and colleagues, *Negotiating Cultures: Eugenio Barba and the Intercultural Debate* (Manchester: Manchester University Press, 2002), pp. 142–58.

11 Sources of inspiration

The second season began about three years after I joined the group. One day Eugenio decided, after having seen my training, that I was now ready to be directly responsible for my work. This is when my training became individual. It was a moment of great freedom but also of great solitude. Up until then my work had been observed regularly by a more senior actor or by Eugenio himself, who would give me the necessary indications and advice.

Now that I had to decide on my own what to do, I needed inspiration.

There are various ways of finding inspiration. For example, by looking at the work of other theatre groups, seeing performances of other theatre traditions, reading books, going to the cinema, or looking at photographs and works of art.

During a tour in Belgrade in 1976 I had the opportunity to see Bob Wilson's *Einstein on the Beach*. I was struck from the very first moment by the performance's particularly slow rhythm, the huge mobile set designs, and the repetitive music of Philip Glass. A dancer who performed a dance-like walk moved towards the spectators in a diagonal line, and then retreated along the same path. The changes were so minimal that after some minutes it only took a slightly bigger change to create a huge impact.

This was a revelation for me. I started to work on the principle of the repetition of movement, introducing pieces by Philip Glass in my training. I tried to imitate what I had seen Bob Wilson's dancer do. I inserted, within a fixed structure – the forward and backward danced walk – minimal variations that mainly consisted of the occasional shifting of emphasis in my steps.

I worked on this principle for years, applying it also to my arms.

I began by clapping my hands rhythmically. Then I explored variations of clapping: the size (from very small to enormous), the speed (from very slow to very fast), and placing the accent (the emphasis) in different parts of the action. The changes in intensity, speed, size and direction could occur not only between one action and another, but also within the same action. Emphasising the moment the hands are about to meet, rather than the one where they have just separated, changed the meaning of the action. It could transform the conjunction of the hands from an act of prayer to the flight of a bird, from applause to a gesture of reproach, from an act of surrender to kneading dough.

A similar process of altering form proved to be very useful in the various interpretations of a score. But I will speak about this later on.

On tour, I took an active part in the workshops led by Eugenio.

4 October 1979
Workshop in Aix en Provence.
We begin with the work on the spine doing bridges, shoulder stands and head stands.

Eugenio says: 'The important thing is not to do the exercise, but to be aware of the process that occurs on a muscular level. Focus your attention on the collaboration between weight and force of gravity.'

Then we proceed to work on the legs. Eugenio says: 'Work on the step, focusing on the movement of the body; the feet, focusing on the way they touch the floor; the knees, focusing on their trajectories that determine directions in the space. Now create three walks: one in water; a decisive one; and one carrying a person on your shoulders. Then work on the different walks and different rhythms.'

Eugenio introduces some music.

5 October 1979
We begin by working on the arms.

Eugenio says: 'Explore the possibilities of movement in the shoulders, the elbows, the wrists. Find three possibilities for every articulation. Then create different combinations of the possibilities that engage the articulations. First, all the possibilities with an arm. Then, with both arms simultaneously. And then, with an arm that performs one possibility and the other performing another possibility.

Eugenio selects one of the participants and goes through this whole process with him while the others observe.

Eugenio asks him to combine the forms he had fixed (the exercises) with the steps he found the previous day.

He tells the participant: 'Do not forget the eyes!'
And then he adds the work on rhythm.

Eugenio says: 'One who walks with a stiff leg gives the impression of being infirm. What we are searching for, on the contrary, is to free ourselves from infirmity. You have to end the action in a precise way that allows you to retain energy and start again in the direction you want. Now insert different directions in what you are doing. Surprise yourself!'
Eugenio asks all the participants to do the same. Then he says: 'This experience cannot be transmitted with words. You cannot transmit what you have learnt. Not even with exercises. You have to accustom the body to think in order to achieve an organic expression instead of artificial acting. There exists a difference in the need: you fly if you want to.'

Books are another source of inspiration for me, not just by means of words but also through images. For example, in art books I can find a plethora of suggestions on how to compose the body. In the course of centuries, painters and sculptors have chosen the poses of their models with care, which were then immortalised in their work.

During a tour in France in the early 1980s I came across a photography book on the game of *boules: Pétanque et jeu provençal*.[1] It contained images which portrayed various moments of the game played by elderly people. In these images I could perceive that in the moment they prepared to throw a *boule*, the players thought with all of their body. To accomplish a *bocciata* (a hit), that is to displace an adversary's *boule* from its advantageous position and leave yours closer to the jack, the players had to accumulate an exact amount of energy. To obtain the desired result they had to involve the body as a whole, not just the arm and the hand.

I was fascinated by their presence, frozen in the photographs, and I tried to create an equivalent within my physical training.

What struck me about those photographs was the fact that they fixed a movement. So I began by throwing an imaginary *boule* in different directions in the space, freezing the action at the moment the *boule* left my hand. In doing the action I gave myself the task to maintain balance on the ball of one foot.

If, while throwing a *boule* to my left, I allow the weight of my body to follow the same direction of my arm, I will fall accordingly. To stay balanced I have to create a counter-impulse: for example, with the right side of my torso. However, if this in turn is too strong, my body will fall in that direction. That is why I have to calculate, simultaneously, both the strength of the throw and that of the counter-impulse.

Balance is always the result of two opposite but equivalent forces.

I can throw the imaginary *boule* in different directions in the space, slowly or rapidly, gently or forcefully, with small or big movements.

Examples of throws.

The impulse for the throw can be slow and gentle, and then the *boule* can be thrown in a rapid and energetic manner. Being an integral part of the action, the impulse can undergo variations of speed and intensity. The end of each throw contains the *sats* for the start of the next one. Modulating my energy in space and time, I create a flow: a continuous and varied flux of energy.

My training has grown according to changes, undergoing continuous transformation in the process. Its development has been caused by choosing to do what at that moment appeared most functional to my professional growth.

At some times the changes were suggested by Eugenio. At others they were produced by the exploration of new principles. On occasion they were even suggested by the introduction of texts, objects or music while working on a principle that had already been explored for quite some time and had become less challenging.

During a tour in Japan in 1979 I bought a little hat adorned with paper flowers. I decided to use it in my composition training, which at that time was going through a period of stagnation. As soon as I put it on I had the sensation that it was the hat itself that was dancing with my legs. The work changed thanks to the new images that arose in my mind, and slowly a dance took shape.

During the same tour in Japan I heard the Japanese *taiko* drums for the first time, and I used some recordings of them in a part of my training. I directed my eyes rhythmically to different directions in the space to the sound of this percussion and I moved with walks or movements that had a dynamic which did not belong to either my cultural roots or the training I had done up until that moment. The music generated a new scenic behaviour in me and, like the hat, made me discover new 'gold veins' in my training.

Note

1   Hans Silvester, *Pétanque et jeu provençal* (Paris: Chêne, 1977). Photographs by Hans Silvester and text by Yvan Audouard.

12 Dialogue with tiredness

I am convinced that in every one of us there is a well of energy from which we very rarely draw, and then only in extreme circumstances. A voluntary confrontation of situations that push us beyond exhaustion allows us to find the way towards that well from which we draw the energy we need to replenish our scenic presence.

The first two seasons of my training included acrobatic, 'Swiss', physical and plastique exercises, work on the principles of composition, introversion/extroversion and slow motion, as well as dances with sticks and wands. I focused on each of these for at least twenty to thirty minutes. This extended time allowed me to meet, daily, a very faithful companion: exhaustion. I became tired. I felt that I had reached my limits and I was tempted to give in to the desire to stop. At that point I asked myself: what lies beyond exhaustion, beyond my immediate limits? What happens if I continue for three minutes more?

The presence of Eugenio in the training space (with his eyes and comments) and the other companions (by their example) helped me to explore this possibility for years. By not stopping and continuing to work, I superseded the moment of impasse and extended my limits. With the passing of time and experience I understood that physical training is, in fact, mental training. Those who do sports, like those who go jogging, know this very well.

Armed with a brand new pair of running shoes and full of good intentions, we decide to go jogging one fine morning. After about fifteen minutes the body becomes heavy and starts to ache. But if we are with someone who has been jogging for a long time, we manage to keep going. All of a sudden the body feels lighter after some minutes. What has happened? The brain starts to produce endorphins – a chemical substance that helps the body to overcome extraordinary challenges. This is what happened to me when I went running with Jens during my first mornings at Odin Teatret in April 1974.

It is possible to dance for hours – at a carnival, a wedding or a village feast – and feel exhausted without being tired. In fact, if your favourite song comes on at the end, you cannot resist the temptation to start dancing again. On the other hand, it is possible to feel terribly tired – or even fall asleep – during the first fifteen minutes of a conference.

Which tires first, the body or the mind? As far as I am concerned, it is the mind. The boredom generated by the mechanical execution of exercises and fixed scores of actions is exhausting and leads to the temptation to surrender. So, while training I have to keep the mind occupied by thinking about the following elements:

- space, the directions I move in and the lines I follow: straight, curved or serrated;
- energy, the intensity of the action;
- speed, the tempo and rhythm;
- dimension, the size of the action.

In this way I generate a context that allows my mind to project images onto the grey wall of boredom as well as give the action I am performing other meanings to which I then react.

Apart from keeping my attention alive, the flow of these images is essential for the work with principles or sequences of exercises because it provides a dynamic charged with nuances and variations. It is these kinds of images that I use later on in the creation of improvisations and the interpretation of scores.

Transcending the state of exhaustion is the result of an effort of will that, on the one hand, accustoms us not to give up at the first hurdle (thus exceeding our immediate limits), and on the other hand is proof of the authenticity of the actor's motivation.

I often mention to my students the example of great pianists who had to practise for very long periods before feeling ready to play famous musical pieces. Apart from developing their technique and motor ability (reading a note means pressing a specific key for a determined length of time and with a set intensity), the daily work on scales and arpeggios also tests their motivation.

As Eugenio said in Aix en Provence: 'You fly if you want to'.

Our training is not aimed at specialisation. I can learn Japanese dances without becoming a Nihon Buyo dancer. I can play the cello in a performance without being a cellist. However, this does not mean that the moment I master, say, four acrobatic exercises I move on to do something else.

I have often discovered that new light is shed on an old principle when I return to it after working on other principles.

In my opinion, one of the essential functions of training is to retain the capacity to learn.

13 Segmentation

The principle of segmentation marked a change of direction in my training.
With daily repetition we learn to work so well with a principle that our body risks engaging what I call the 'automatic pilot'. The mind thinks of something else while the body repeats, for the umpteenth time, a fixed sequence of actions. Instead of reinvigorating us, this split between the mind and the body generates exhaustion. If it happens for many days in succession, it means that it is time to introduce objects or explore new principles in the training.
I was in the second season of my training in the early 1980s and for eight years I had been committed to filling the space with energy. In the course of time, my work on some principles became automatic: my body could do the exercises on its own. It was as if the work was drifting along with the same flow I had long fought to achieve. It was time to break the clichés I had built in my work during years of training and performances. And it was precisely in training that I had the opportunity of searching for new ways of compelling my mind to dance with my body, and vice versa.
I had to find a way that impeded me from moving involuntarily. As part of my daily training I decided to sit down on a chair and explore the possibilities that emerged from this new situation. I found a sea of opportunities.
I worked by moving one joint at a time, controlling every little detail up to the point of deciding whether to focus my eyes five, ten, or even a hundred metres in front of me.
I set myself the rule to move only one part or my body at a time – the eyes, the head, the arms, the torso – keeping the rest of the body completely immobile. I decided that even the eyes were an articulation. I called this principle 'segmentation'.

The principle of segmentation: 'I move one joint at a time, keeping the rest of the body immobile.'

I can move my eyes to the left, and then turn my head in the same direction. I can turn my head to the right keeping my eyes looking to the left, and then move them to the right. I can also move my eyes and head simultaneously, but only if I decide to do so beforehand.

The difficulty is to keep the rest of the body completely immobile.

Nothing must happen automatically or involuntarily.

Our body, which is not accustomed to moving one joint at a time, has the tendency to move many parts simultaneously. Therefore, when working with this principle, I have to consciously perform the action of keeping my body immobile and move only the selected joint.

I can, for example, lift the arm starting from the shoulder; move the hand close to the chest by bending the elbow; bend the wrist upward; bend three fingers downward; lift the arm starting from the shoulder until the index finger touches my lips.

I do not execute a sequence which has been fixed in advance. I have to establish in the moment *which* joint to move and *how* to do it. In this continuous improvisation I consciously decide the phrasing of every movement, that is, I choose how to modulate my energy. It is important to vary the speed of these changes. Indeed, one of the challenges of this principle is to avoid the staccato rhythm that tends to accompany the movement of isolated articulations, which produces the unwanted result of a puppet-like body.

If, as I have already said, a principle is a frame of rules that limits my freedom and forces me to work in depth, then the principle of segmentation is the smallest frame within which I have trained.

Sometimes I found myself in positions that were totally unknown to me. At other times I would find a daily position by means of an unusual route. All the gestures and final positions were between the limits of the daily and the abstract.

By moving one articulation at a time in a continuous improvisation, one can end up with actions that belong to daily life, for example, combing: starting from the shoulder, I lift my arm above my head; I close my fingers, one joint at a time; starting from the elbow, I lower the hand until it touches my head; starting from the shoulder, I lower my arm, sliding 'the comb' through my hair.

To keep training on segmentation even while touring I needed a folding chair, so I bought a deck chair. After three years of working on this principle, some images began to take shape in my mind and a panorama appeared in front of my eyes.

Among the first images that emerged was that of a beach. But which beach? Who was I? What was I doing there?

At the time I was using the music of Erik Satie in my training – it provided me with the feeling of time passing which, engrossed as I was in the work, would otherwise have gone unnoticed. The first beach to appear in my mind was the one on the Lido di Venezia at the beginning of the twentieth century. My movements were slow and measured; perhaps I was an upper class lady. I was on my own on the beach, so it could not have been summer. If I was there out of season I must have been ill. I thought of James Joyce, who had lived in Trieste for a long period. Lucia, his daughter, was schizophrenic. That's it: I had a mental illness. I always kept my hair in a plait during training. Early twentieth-century women wore their hair up in a full bun. Instead, I decided that a woman with a mental illness would wear her hair loose, as in the Japanese Noh theatre tradition. So from that moment onwards I left my hair untied during the work on segmentation and began to explore its possibilities as I had done with every other part of my body. My hair had a life of its own that followed the force of gravity. I could make it slide in various ways down the back of the chair if I moved slowly forward. If I moved even further I could make it fall to the floor. If I moved a handheld fan rapidly in front of my face, my hair flew upwards in disarray.

The image which gradually began to take shape was that of a sick young lady waiting on a beach. The waiting evoked a new figure in me: Penelope.

These images emerged spontaneously in situations of training.

At the time I was reading James Joyce's *Ulysses* where, in the final chapter, Molly Bloom awaits her Ulysses, like Penelope. I memorised her monologue in order to have a text that could accompany my actions, and so give more substance to the 'ghost' of this character who was taking shape.

The principle of segmentation is not, by itself, an absolute guarantee that leads you to achieve a specific quality of presence. As with the work on any other principle, the risk of being 'mechanical' and 'lifeless' exists even in this case. However, over time the sequences of actions that kept reappearing during my work with the chair generated a specific quality of presence. From this physical way of behaving sprang an imaginary world within which I started to act.

When I saw *Apocalypse Now*, the images of napalm rain setting alight the Vietnamese jungle to the sound of 'The End' by The Doors had a strong impact on me. The mental landscape that encompassed the work on segmentation changed from that moment onwards. It was no longer simply a beach where crabs moved around my feet and I reacted by withdrawing my legs, nor was it where I outlined in the sand the shadow of the man I was waiting for and who, appearing behind me, made me get up from my deck chair, hesitantly rising to my feet. Now I also saw the flaming jungle on the horizon. I began to react consciously to these images with my gaze. My eyes, which up until then had been focusing on a relatively nearby zone, began to look at the horizon with a new intensity. My panorama grew in size and depth.

I did not use the image of the jungle in flames simply because I wanted to create a specific effect with the eyes, but rather because I had seen a film which had moved me profoundly. At the same time, I was also aware of the fact that this kind of work made the look in my eyes more alive.

There is always a subtle balance between what one chooses to do consciously and what happens by chance.

In the course of time, this character sitting on a deck chair took the name 'Dama Bianca' (The White Lady).

After years of working with the principle of segmentation, I found that I could use it to create a kind of theatrical 'close-up'.

When film directors want the audience to see the hand of an actor, they ask the camera operator to shoot at close-up range. In this way, at a specific moment the audience will be faced with a ten-by-five-metre hand that is impossible to miss.

How can a close-up be created in a theatrical situation, where spectators can look wherever they want? The director can direct the public's attention by using a spotlight to pick out the actor's hand, leaving the rest of the scene in darkness. But one can also explore other possibilities.

The spectator's gaze falls instinctively on the actor's eyes. Of course, the audience sees the face in full just as they see the rest of the body and most of the scene, but they instinctively look at the actor's eyes. So, if I want spectators to focus their attention on my hand, I lower my eyes, I keep the rest of my body completely immobile and allow only my hand to move.

I found the principle of segmentation to be particularly useful in performances where I am alone on stage and in those where, compared to group performances, the spectator has fewer possibilities of choosing where to look.

The opening scene of *Judith* was built around this principle. In this scene the spectator's attention is made to dance within a limited space: sitting on a deck chair, I move one segment of the body at a time, letting the text come to the fore. If the text is very important, the actions have to be restrained in order not to distract the spectator from the meaning of the words. This is also the case when the actions underline or comment on the text. I will come back later to the influence of the segmentation principle on the creation of *Judith*.

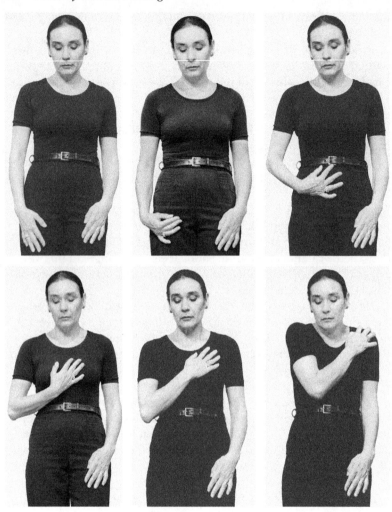

In a theatrical 'close-up', the eyes are lowered and the body is immobile while only the hand moves.

14 Being decided

By means of training, over the years the distance between thought and action is progressively reduced until they become one. It is then that the actor becomes 'decided'.

Being decided is an essential quality which allows us to react in an appropriate manner on stage, even in unforeseen circumstances: an object falls, an actor stumbles and loses balance. Eugenio taught us that in these cases we need to react promptly by picking up and dropping the object again, not once but twice; by standing up and falling again, twice over. In this way the spectator does not realise that it was an accident and thinks that the action was intentional.

There is a big difference between, on the one hand, thinking an action and then doing it, and on the other hand, being one with the action.

An action is different from a movement. A movement does not aim physically to change something in the space. An action always wants to produce a change. I shift my notebook: this is an action. I want to change the position of my notebook – that is, I have a precise intention. If it were a suitcase instead of a notebook, then my *in-tension* would be different because my body would have to prepare to lift a heavier weight.

Every action is in fact a reaction to a thought, a need, a sound, or another person's action. A reaction always has a precise *in-tension* that directly influences the muscular tonicity of the body – but first of all, the eyes. I still remember clearly how it needed only a glance from my mother to stop my hand in its journey towards the pastry tray that was waiting for the guests to arrive. Her look, in reaction to my intention, became action.

The Italian word for 'intention' – *intenzione* – alludes to an internal tension. I see it as a tension in my 'snake' with my eyes as its head. The decision to shift the eyes in a specific direction influences the behaviour of my spine.

Audiences are often bored when they foresee what is about to happen; that is, when they recognise the actor's intention before it is executed as an action. This happens when an actor recalls an action that needs to be done and prepares mentally to perform it an instant before actually doing it.

In our profession, training accustoms us to be present in the moment. It also compels us to be unpredictable by means of changes in *sats*. Moreover, training accustoms us to change the meaning of an action by altering its *in-tension*. A raised hand in the act of a caress can transform into the first stage of a slap.

When I work on a scene, I do not think in terms of categories of slow and fast but according to images. For example, if during a scene I have to lower myself to pick up a notebook from the floor, I will not look immediately at the object. I will first look to my right and then to my left before I kneel. My aim is to avoid anticipating the action, while at the same time justifying what I do by giving it a logical reason: I look around me to make sure that I am not being seen by anyone, or maybe to ask myself why no one has picked up the notebook yet, perhaps even to check if there are other objects on the floor that need picking up. I look at the notebook only in the last instant, and then I kneel. At this point I can choose to use the *in-tension* of picking it up as if it were a feather, lifting it up with two fingers.

The important thing for me is not to do an action mechanically by following the shortest route as we do in daily life, but rather to evoke – by means of phrasing – images that change my *in-tension* and awaken, in the mind of spectators, associations that offer various levels of interpretation.

The actor needs to know how to direct the spectator's attention to keep their interest alive.

I define the actor's work as a 'dance of intentions'.

15 Thought in action

I started taking guitar lessons as soon as I arrived in Carpignano. A year later I began to study the violin, but I had to abandon this instrument because I was asked to play a five-string banjo for *Come! And the Day Will be Ours*. Four years later I started studying the cello, and at the same time Eugenio asked me to learn to play drums. The cello became part of the chamber orchestra in *Brecht's Ashes*[1] and the drums part of the orchestra in *The Million*.[2]

Playing an instrument was part of my daily training during my first ten years at Odin Teatret. This form of training had a lot of things in common with my physical training. By developing my motor abilities, I had to learn how to transform my intentions into sound. It also taught me how to listen.

After months of exercise I could interpret a musical score by focusing on its phrasing and playing with a certain flow. However, playing with other people required being connected through a shared sense of rhythm.

Keeping a rhythm requires being present in the instant, so learning how to play the drums was excellent training for me to achieve this end. The 'beat' is here and now; if you think the beat before you do it, the result will be a perfect 'after beat'. In the case of drums, where all the limbs are involved, playing means listening with your ears and reacting with the rest of the body.

December 1995 marked the beginning of the final year of performing *Kaosmos*.[3] In order to prepare myself for the creation of a new performance, for which Eugenio had already given us the first indications, I felt the need to 'wash away' the form of scenic presence of my *Kaosmos* character. To this end I chose to learn a new dance: flamenco. I was intrigued by the ability of a flamenco dancer's body to become a musical instrument capable of giving life to complex rhythms. The feet beat the floor or hardly touch it, voluminous skirts are made to fly by the knees, the arms spin gracefully and forcefully, while the hands clap the rhythm and seal the energy in the upper part of the body with precise accents.

During my first lessons I realised that there are two opposing tensions in the body of a flamenco dancer: the lower part tends downwards, towards the earth, while the upper part tends upwards, towards the sky. This reminded me of the basic *in-tension* of Nihon Buyo that Katsuko Azuma had taught me.[4] Furthermore, in both dances, the shoulders are held low while the nape of the neck is extended and exposed in the process. However, in comparison with the straight spine of the Nihon Buyo dancer, in flamenco the back is arched.

This architecture of *in-tensions* creates a formalised scenic presence. Learning flamenco compelled me, once again, to be present in the instant with all my body. Every hesitation is exposed by moments of imprecise rhythm.

Eugenio tried on various occasions to insert flamenco dances and steps during the rehearsals of *Mythos*,[5] but to no avail: the performance rejected them like foreign bodies. Nevertheless, the basic position of Cassandra, my character in *Mythos*, holds her back arched and her solemn gait has the quality of a 'horse pawing the ground', both of which derived from my experience with flamenco.

In order to proceed with my narrative, I need to leap back in time once again.

When I joined Odin Teatret in 1974 the actors trained with a wooden stick, which was one metre eighty centimetres long with a diameter of four centimetres. They called it the 'bushman' and I worked with it as well. Eugenio asked us to create exercises that had a precise beginning, a middle and an end. The rule was that we always had to hold the stick from the middle or at one of the ends. When we threw the stick in the air and had to catch it again at one of the ends, it invariably inclined towards the floor. We therefore had to make a precise physical effort to hold it parallel to the floor. This was relatively easy for the others, but for me, who had just arrived from the benches of the university, it was a very hard task to accomplish.

The work with the bushman formed part of our collective training. At Odin Teatret there has never been a difference between the training for males and the training for females. Everyone worked on the same principles in the first years. Then, with time, the actors' training became individualised.

When I joined the group, every actor had chosen how to decorate their own bushman, how to paint it or adorn it with coloured tape. It was from the training with this object that *The Book of Dances* later emerged in Carpignano.

After about three years of training and improvisation with the bushman and the 'little torches', I was allowed to use a walking stick with a knob.

The fact that I started with a big stick and then moved on to a smaller one might appear strange. It seems more logical to do it the other way round. However, a smaller stick, which is lighter, would not have offered the resistance that I needed. I could assess my strength more easily if I had to confront a precise resistance.

I began by repeating the exercises I had done with the bushman, imagining that the walking stick was just as heavy. Then I abandoned these exercises and started to improvise freely. Due to the reduced dimensions of the new object, the dynamic that developed between the walking stick and my body was different from the one with the bushman. This new dynamic evoked images that I could recognise – for example, a sword, an arch, an arrow, and a bird.

It is very important to understand that these images emerged gradually from a physical commitment by means of a process that I define as 'thought in action'. That is, I did not first think the images and then recreate them with the body. On the contrary, my mind recognised the images created during the movement by means of the body-stick unity. When this happened, I named the image and wrote it down in my work diary: warrior, sword, parasol, oar, fishing rod, golf club, aiming the arrow, firing the arrow, injured bird, fall in the lake...

Once I had accumulated a number of images, I could then mount them together in a succession of scenes. Here is an example:

- There is a *warrior* in the woods.
- He hears a sound and unsheathes his *sword*. 'Who goes there?'
- Ah, it is only a lady who is walking on the river bank with her *parasol*.
- An old man is *rowing* a boat in the middle of the river.
- He is out angling with his *fishing rod*.
- When the fish swallows the bait, he *pulls it out from the water*,
- and sees some people *playing golf* on the other bank of the river.

- *Looking at the white ball* in mid-air, a child
- *spots* a duck.
- He *aims* at it,
- *fires an arrow* and hits it.
- The *injured duck*
- *falls* in the river.

I do not follow a linear logic to link these images; rather, there is an evocative logic that progresses in leaps of association. This kind of logic, which I developed in training, also became useful during my improvisations for performances.

Notes

1 *Brecht's Ashes*, first version: 1980–82, second version: 1982–84. A performance dedicated to Jens Bjørneboe. Actors: Torben Bjelke (only in the first version), Roberta Carreri, Toni Cots, Tom Fjordefalk (only in the first version), Tage Larsen, Francis Pardeilhan, Iben Nagel Rasmussen, Silvia Ricciardelli, Ulrik Skeel, Julia Varley and Torgeir Wethal. Text and direction: Eugenio Barba.
2 *The Million*, 1978–84. A performance dedicated to Marco Polo. Actors: Torben Bjelke, Roberta Carreri, Toni Cots, Tom Fjordefalk, Tage Larsen, Else Marie Laukvik, Francis Pardeilhan, Iben Nagel Rasmussen, Silvia Ricciardelli, Gustavo Riondet, Ulrik Skeel, Julia Varley and Torgeir Wethal (some of the actors participated in only one of the various versions until 1984). Direction: Eugenio Barba.
3 *Kaosmos*, 1993–96. Actors: Kai Bredholt, Roberta Carreri, Jan Ferslev, Tina Nielsen, Iben Nagel Rasmussen, Isabel Ubeda, Julia Varley, Torgeir Wethal and Frans Winther. Dramaturgy and direction: Eugenio Barba.
4 Katsuko Azuma was a master of the classical Japanese dance Nihon Buyo. She was one of the founding members of ISTA in 1979 and participated in the first five sessions held between 1980 and 1987. Azuma died in 1995.
5 *Mythos – Ritual for a Brief Century*, 1998–2005. A performance dedicated to Atahualpa del Cioppo. Actors: Kai Bredholt, Roberta Carreri, Jan Ferslev, Tage Larsen, Iben Nagel Rasmussen, Julia Varley, Torgeir Wethal and Frans Winther. Dramaturgy and direction: Eugenio Barba.

Thought in action 73

There is a warrior in the woods.

He hears a sound and unsheathes his sword. 'Who goes there?'

Ah, it is only a lady who is walking on the river bank with her parasol.

An old man is rowing a boat in the middle of the river.

Thought in action 75

He is out angling with his fishing rod. When the fish swallows the bait, he pulls it out from the water...

... and sees some people playing golf on the other bank of the river.

Looking at the white ball in mid-air, a child spots a duck. He aims at it…

… fires an arrow and hits it.

Thought in action 77

The injured duck...

...falls in the river.

16 Improvisations

Improvisation is as much part of training as it is of a performance's creation process.

I know three different types:

1 Improvisation *with fixed elements*. Starting from a given chain of exercises or a sequence of actions, I can improvise with the dynamics and order of parts. In this way I become accustomed to interpreting physical scores; that is, using fixed sequences of actions to react to the work of a colleague, or applying them to a text.
2 Improvisation *within the parameters of a principle*. I can do whatever I want as long as I stick to the rules of a given principle. Here the scope of improvisation is even wider in that one does not start by learning a fixed form, but by improvising within the frame of a principle to explore different possibilities.

 With daily repetition a sequence of actions gradually emerges and is fixed, and it is then used as a fresh point of departure to improvise with different dynamics.
3 Improvisation *starting from a theme*. To create material for performances, I follow the flow of associations that emerge from a theme that is usually given by Eugenio.

 This type of improvisation needs a fuller explanation and yet another leap backwards in time.

I had never done any theatre before joining Odin Teatret.

I had hardly crossed the threshold of the theatre on my arrival in Holstebro in April 1974 when Iben took me to her dressing-room and made me wear a rust-coloured tunic of coarse cotton. The lights were low in the white room where Eugenio and the other actors were waiting. I sat on a bench like the others. Eugenio started to speak in Norwegian, a language I did not know. He

Improvisations 79

whispered something to Iben who moved towards the centre of the room. I deciphered what she did as an *improvisation*. I had never seen anyone improvise in my life. All the other actors followed suit, one at a time.

At one point Eugenio turned to me and said: 'You are in the king's garden. You are afraid. But someone holds your hand and it becomes light.' I was very afraid. I stood up and moved forward in the empty space. I closed my eyes and began to move slowly. I remember clearly the feeling of the wooden floor under my feet: it was the only thing that I could hold on to. The images that the theme had evoked in me evaporated quickly but I kept moving all the same. I was afraid that if I stopped too soon Eugenio would think that I was not clever enough. When I opened my eyes I found myself looking at the weak light of a lamp.

I still remember the beginning of that first improvisation of mine. Starting from the theme provided by Eugenio, I mentally decided on a sequence of images that I then reproduced physically: I am strolling in the king's garden, I see a flower, I pick it and place it behind my ear, it begins to rain...

If I had done that improvisation a year or two later, equipped with the experience acquired in the meantime, I would have been guided not only by the descriptive logic of the images, but also by the logic that proceeds through leaps of associations and which allows me to respond through actions to the mental images awakened by my own actions.

I would have followed this internal dialogue: 'No one is allowed in the king's garden. I shouldn't be here. I have to be very careful not to make any noise in order to avoid being caught by surprise. I see a beautiful flower and want to pick it, but I have to make sure that no one is looking. When I move close to the flower, to smell its perfume, hundreds of little warriors spring from the flower and hit me with their swords. They also leap out from all the other flowers, and they injure me. But it starts to rain and every drop is a little angel who, with their big wings, crush the little warriors. And so the rain saves me.'

No one is allowed in the king's garden. I shouldn't be here. I have to be very careful not to make any noise in order to avoid being caught by surprise. I see a beautiful flower and want to pick it, but I have to make sure that no one is looking.

Improvisations 81

When I move close to the flower, to smell its perfume, hundreds of little warriors spring from the flower and hit me with their swords. They also leap out from all the other flowers, and they injure me.

But it starts to rain and every drop is a little angel who, with their big wings, crushes the little warriors. And so the rain saves me.

17 Individual improvisation

I have been told that at the beginning of Odin Teatret Eugenio worked on what he called the 'psychophysical'. This was a training aimed at learning how to do physical improvisations. Even though I have never heard Eugenio speak of the 'psychophysical', I remember that during the first years of my apprenticeship he would regularly make me do improvisations which were not aimed at the creation of a performance, and so were never filmed.

These improvisations were not held on a daily basis because, as Eugenio told us, there was the risk of draining away the personal well from which we draw our material for performances.

Eugenio and the other companions often advised me on how to improvise. They told me, for example, to follow an internal film when doing an improvisation. This was an evocative direction, but one which nonetheless demanded a mental technique that I still did not possess. It took me years of training to learn how to embody the images that emerge in my mind. However, there were also other difficulties that hampered my capacity to improvise.

Once, in 1975, during the creation of *Come! And the Day Will be Ours*, Eugenio gave me a theme that reminded me of a disappointed love. During the improvisation I allowed myself to get emotionally carried away and I even burst out crying. After a break, Eugenio commented that the improvisation had not worked and he asked me to try again. I was desperate. I started again, this time by doing the action of imagining peeling skin from all over my body. At the end of the second improvisation Eugenio said: 'This is all right'.

My work as an actress always draws on my lived experience, whether real or imaginary, and as such, by definition it is personal and thus private. However, in the work space we use the word 'private' in a negative sense to indicate a kind of behaviour that belongs to daily life, and which does not contain the necessary formalised scenic behaviour needed to render it theatrical.

In the case of the first improvisation, where I was inspired by the memory of my grief, I got carried away by a bout of self-pity which prevented me from dramatising what I was doing. On the other hand, the decision to be led by the image of peeling skin compelled me to a precision that rendered my action true: I translated sorrow into a physical action.

Over the years, 'formalised scenic behaviour' has become second nature to Odin Teatret actors.

The improvisations that contribute to the creation of performances are, with some exceptions in the case of *My Father's House* and *The Gospel According to Oxyrhincus*,[1] always individual, and they depend on a theme as a point of departure. The theme that Eugenio gives us is never directly linked with the scene we are rehearsing at the time. Some of the themes I have been given include 'Cognac runs in my veins' and 'Like a cheetah on Kilimanjaro snow'.

From my work diary:

Holstebro, October 1981
The work on Brecht's Ashes *continues. Eugenio said: 'There is something you know very well and it is that your expression is "in spite of yourself". If the theme that I give you for an improvisation does not correspond to the context in which it will be placed, it is in order to protect our work. In life we do not think about expressing anything, except when we simulate something. This also happens to me in the creation of a performance: I express something in spite of myself. Being "expressive in spite of oneself" is a problem for the actor.*

'What we call "kraft training" (strong training) is a way of working without "acting". The kind of improvisation that we use in training is also very useful for improvisation in performances. There is always something that ruins your training: the mouth opens, the arms move symmetrically, the work with the eyes is missing ... You are now concentrating a lot on movement. True training is not in movement but in immobility. Stops are the most important thing. As from today, fifteen minutes of your training should be done sitting down.

'There are three parts of the body that decide: eyes, hands, wrists. In training you hold them in a straight line, but they should be zigzag. The actor has to breathe from the wrists and the knees. At the Comédie Française, when the actors walked, the arms had to be aligned with the legs, contrary to what they do naturally. The hands could never be held lower than the waist. When they pointed, the arms could never be held lower than the head.

'Now I would like to try an experiment with you: do your training with a blindfold on.'
We do so.
'The eyes construct the space. You have to follow rules; for example, in classical ballet the rule is that the eyes should always follow the hands.'
Iben: *'I can't take training with you anymore. Eugenio comes to the work space to talk, and not to listen to the actor. I feel like someone who plays classical music in the midst of people who play rock. It's like training in a marketplace.'*
Eugenio: *'Grotowski told me how everything that up to now has been done in secret, now takes place in the square. I know that I have to do something concrete for my actors. It is my role. Do not confuse the nostalgia of the relationship you had with me when you were "children" with the relationship that I now have with you as "adults".'*

Between 1964 and 1972, all the actors used to be present in the work space and had the task of noting down the improvisation of a companion. The aim was to help the actor repeat the improvisation later on. It was a process that required patience, but in the span of three or four hours, the actor was able to memorise the improvisation with their companion's assistance.

From 1972 onwards, improvisations were filmed in the presence of Eugenio and the cameraman, who was usually Torgeir. This was the customary procedure by the time I joined the group.

After an improvisation, I would watch it on the screen with Eugenio who would either indicate fragments for me to memorise or ask me to learn it in its entirety. Learning a five-minute improvisation would sometimes require a week because the video, unlike the memory of colleagues, reproduced every detail faithfully. When I was in a position to repeat it, I would show the improvisation to Eugenio who would watch it over and over again so that he could then elaborate it. For example, he would ask me to reduce some actions or change the direction of others; sometimes he would create a new sequence, mounting a series of fragments in a completely different order than the original one. The result was like a little Frankenstein, completely lacking in organicity. After a day or two and a lot of repetition, I would be able to breathe life into my actions by re-establishing, internally, another logic that justified and linked the new montage.

At this point Eugenio could decide to insert the work directly into a scene of the performance or involve another actor. In the case of the latter, he would ask both of us to create a 'dialogue' with our improvisations, taking turns to perform one action at a time. Eugenio would observe the work at length, seeking out points of connection. He would then modify some of our actions, asking us to change the speed, direction and size, in the process creating relationships from which other meanings would then emerge. Slowly he would give shape to a new scene which, when inserted in the new performance, acquired a meaning that none of us could have foreseen.

Eugenio does not have preconceived ideas about the end result of an improvisation. He too needs to be surprised to avoid the automatisms of his own thought processes.

Let us consider the hypothetical example of a scene in one of our performances where an evil emperor wants to sentence a young and noble warrior to death. To this end, the emperor summons all the church and army leaders to his court. If I had to play the character of the young warrior, Eugenio would ask me to use one of my physical scores.

I could use the second version of my improvisation 'In the King's Garden'. The slow walk which I originally used to enter cautiously in the garden is justifiable in this scene because a man with a death sentence on his head walks slowly to savour every moment of life. In the improvisation I looked around to make sure no one would see me pick the flower; in the performance I could use the same action to look at all those who are about to sentence me to death. The action of going down on my knees to pick up the flower could become, in the performance, the act of kneeling in front of the emperor.

Every action is transposed directly, and faithfully, from the improvisation. At the same time I also need to modify slightly the original dynamics of my *in-tensions* to give them a meaning that makes sense in relation to the new context. On the other hand, I have to be careful not to adjust my new *in-tensions* to the point where they become merely illustrative, thereby making them lose the rich texture that renders them so full of meaning.

One must avoid making an action obvious. At the same time one must also avoid rendering an action incomprehensible. On stage, the space of improvisation that an actor has is that of the interpretation of the score.

The actor has to seduce (*se-ducere*, to lead to oneself) the mind of the spectator, leading him or her to that moment of gratification that consists in understanding what is 'really' happening.

Note

1   *The Gospel According to Oxyrhincus*, 1985–87. Actors: Roberta Carreri, Tage Larsen, Else Marie Laukvik, Francis Pardeilhan, Julia Varley and Torgeir Wethal. Dramaturgy and direction by Eugenio Barba.

Individual improvisation 87

Some fragments from my improvisation 'In the King's Garden' are used in a new context. Top: A young, noble warrior sentenced to death by the emperor, enters the throne room. He walks slowly to savour every moment of life that remains. Bottom: He looks at all those who are about to sentence him and kneels in front of the emperor.

18 Composing a character

Up to 1976 Eugenio always attended the daily sessions of our training. Then he limited his presence to those occasions when an actor felt the need to show him something important or when we needed advice.

His comments were of the utmost importance to me, even if I did not always know how to put them immediately into practice. This was not due to an obscure way of speaking on his part. It was just that my body needed more time than my mind to understand his requests. When he observed the training, Eugenio gave a lot of directions which I then tried to apply immediately and all in one go. I ended up confusing myself in the process. It would take me months to transform his requests into visible results.

In the late 1970s Eugenio returned for a period to observe the daily training. This happened when we started researching the life and works of Bertolt Brecht, a process which gave birth to two performances at the same time: *The Million* and *Brecht's Ashes*.

At that time we used to dedicate a couple of hours of our daily training to what we called *Fiskedam*, which in Danish means a breeding pool for fish. It was there that the little ideas of every actor found the ideal conditions for growth and where Eugenio could fish for those that he needed.

We were given the freedom to work on whatever we wanted. There was space even for the craziest ideas, such as roller skating, unicycling, wearing green or red wigs, dressing up and taking photographs. To accompany each other's work with songs and music, we used trumpets and saxophones, electric bass, accordions, and drums – all instruments which we learnt to play at Holstebro's school of music. For the first time ever in our history we used an amplification system and microphones. Apart from the usual training clothes, in the *Fiskedam* we also wore the costumes we were proposing for our characters. The character of Polly Peachum, one of the three I was given by Eugenio for *Brecht's Ashes*, danced with a parasol. For Polly Peachum I had chosen a 1950s evening dress with a very wide skirt and a low-cut back. Five years later Torgeir used this dress as part of the costume for his false messiah in *The Gospel According to Oxyrhincus*.

Looking back I feel that it was precisely the possibility of introducing costumes and objects used in daily life within the training – such as scissors and balls of wool, umbrellas and roller skates – that created a favourable environment for the birth and growth of some of our characters. It was the *Fiskedam* that gave birth to the characters of Katrin and Mother Courage which Iben and Else Marie[1] created for *Brecht's Ashes*.

On the other hand, my proposal for Polly Peachum did not work out. Eugenio thus decided to work individually with me on the figures he had selected: two of them were extracted from the works of Bertolt Brecht (Polly Peachum from *The Threepenny Opera* and Yvette Pottier from *Mother Courage*) and one from his life history (Margarethe Steffin, his secretary and friend). We worked on building the characters, how they walked, sat, spoke, and sang.

For this performance Eugenio asked me to wear very high heels. Up till then I had always worked barefoot in both training and performance. The change in posture induced by wearing high heels probably helped me to avoid the behavioural automatisms I had developed over the years of working barefoot.

When Eugenio asked me to find the walk for Polly Peachum I thought: 'Polly Peachum is the spoilt child of a rich father, a girl who knows what she wants and how to get it. She wants Mack the Knife and she marries him.' I imagined a self-confident person and so walked in a very extroverted way, with the knees open and the pelvis thrust forward.

Eugenio then asked me to find the walk of Yvette Pottier, a prostitute. I have never seen a prostitute walk in an introverted manner, with the head and shoulders bent. A prostitute has to flaunt her wares, so I imagined that she also walked in an extroverted way, with the knees open and the pelvis thrust forward.

But, of course, it was not possible to have two characters walking in exactly the same manner.

When I showed Eugenio Yvette Pottier's walk, after a couple of steps, he asked me to walk in the opposite manner. So I walked with legs and back introverted while keeping the head and eyes extroverted. Eugenio complicated the composition even further when he told me to refrain from letting the left heel touch the floor.

Two examples of composing a character: Yvette Pottier, completely extroverted; Polly Peachum, the top part of the body is extroverted, and the lower part is introverted.

My Polly Peachum began as a self-confident girl who walked stiffly, and ended up as a complex and sinister character, with a more physically engaging presence, a limp and a curved back. There are many things that are not written in theatre pieces: it is not mentioned that Polly Peachum was lame, but maybe she was.

At this point Eugenio started to work on the facial masks of Polly and Yvette. In one scene of the performance he asked me to give Polly's face the expression of an aggressive wolf, in another the air of teasing superiority.

Our Polly Peachum was born in this way.

The work on the composition of a character also includes research into the way the voice is used. Polly Peachum and Yvette Pottier did not speak: they sang. Margarethe Steffin spoke. From the vocal material I had prepared, Eugenio chose for Margarethe a kind of singsong typical of the way in which memorised texts are recited at school: just like that of an obedient pupil.

After the brief period of the *Fiskedam*, training reverted to the usual mode of collective solitude. Even on tour, in the mornings, we would share the same space where we would be performing in the evening, to work individually. Still, the creative freedom I had experimented with in the *Fiskedam* never left me.

In time I came to define training as 'the secret garden of the actor' – that is, the place where dreams and professional nostalgia can be cultivated, thus exploring all that is important for the actor but which does not find a place in ensemble performances.

In the 1980s Eugenio saw my training once a year or even every two years. The absence of his comments allowed me to develop ideas and work-material with objects and music that emerged from my needs and which required time to mature. In the third stage of my training I cultivated new plants in my 'secret garden'.

We presented the first version of *Brecht's Ashes* from 1980 to 1982, and in the midst of this intense work period, Francis's and my daughter Alice was born, on 25 August 1981.

Note

1 In the end Else Marie Laukvik did not perform in *Brecht's Ashes*.

19 A little digression into private life

'Are you a commune?' 'Do you all live together in the theatre?' I have heard these questions countless times over the years.

No, Odin Teatret is not a commune. It has never been one, even if once, in the early 1970s, there was a moment when Eugenio cherished the idea of buying a farmhouse big enough to house his family and actors. This proposal was not universally accepted in the group and so it did not have a practical outcome. During the first years Judy, Eugenio's English wife, collaborated in the organisation of the theatre. After the birth of their two children she concentrated on translating our performance texts, programme notes and Eugenio's articles and books into English.

In the early years Eugenio had prohibited intimate relationships between members of the group. I do not know who broke this commandment first, but on my arrival in 1974 Torgeir and Iben were separating after some years of cohabitation and two years of marriage. Rune Davide Ricciardelli, the son of Silvia and Torgeir, was born in 1981. In 1977 Tage and Julia married and in 1985 they separated. Francis and I were married in 1978 and we separated in 1982. Francis left the group in 1987. In 1981 Iben married César Brie,[1] and then separated from him in the late 1980s. After living together since 1985 and having the twins Oskar and Victor in 1989, Tage and Anna Lica married in 1993. In the same year Jan Ferslev married Patricia Alves, who eventually became our tour manager for many years; they then separated in 2005. During his first years with Odin Teatret, Ulrik Skeel married a girl from Holstebro with whom he had a child, Christian, and then separated from her some years later. In December 1987, just before he decided to stop being an actor and join our administrative staff, Ulrik married Rina Paglialunga with whom he had just had a child, Anders. Their

Group photo after a training session (1987). Top left: Tage Larsen, Torgeir Wethal, Karl Henrik, Hauch Andersen (technician), Christoph Falke (assistant director), Eugenio Barba, Richard Fowler, César Brie and Ulrik Skeel. Bottom: Else Marie Laukvik, Julia Varley, Roberta Carreri, Iben Nagel Rasmussen, Lena Bjerregaard (wardrobe assistant) and Francis Pardeilhan.

daughter Mariana was born in 1994. Christian Skeel died in 1995. Rina works with Ulrik in the administration of Odin Teatret, and they are still married. In 2010 Kai Bredholt[2] married Erika Sanchez. Else Marie never married.

After living together for twenty-six years since 1983, Torgeir and I got married in 2009.

I will not even mention the other relationships that were not bound by the sacrament of matrimony!

Anyway, we are not a Mormon sect, but nor are we monks.

On returning from Carpignano in 1974 Torgeir rented a big house in Sir, a small village six kilometres from Holstebro. Many members of Odin Teatret, myself included, have lived there. In 1982 Francis and I rented another house in Sir together with Toni, Ulrik, and Walter Ybema.[3] Various combinations of Odin Teatret actors and collaborators have lived in these two houses.

We never contemplated forming a commune. One rents a big house because one likes it, and then chooses the persons with whom to share it, taking turns to do the shopping, cooking, cleaning and mowing the lawn.

The need for privacy increased over the years and various couples relocated to live on their own. Maybe because each of us needed more space to house all the ceramics, paintings and fabrics that we bought while on tour in Latin America.

At a certain point in my life I felt the strong need to be a mother. I think that nothing could have stopped me from becoming one, just as nothing could have impeded me from joining Odin Teatret. These have been the two central choices in my life. I can say that it was not I who made these choices – it was the choices that made me.

Eugenio congratulated me with a smile when I told him about my pregnancy, but I could sense that he was not entirely at ease. It had taken him years to make me an actress of Odin Teatret, and now he was afraid that motherhood might transform me into a housewife. He was afraid that I would privilege my private life at the cost of my loyalty to the work.

These are the facts. I worked until the sixth month of my pregnancy, up to the day contractions began. These contractions forced me to remain under permanent observation in a hospital bed without the possibility of moving from it until Alice's birth. Since Alice was breech, her birth was by Caesarean section with epidural anaesthesia. The following month we began, simultaneously, the rehearsals for a new version of *Brecht's Ashes* and for *The Million* in which I had to insert a new dance.

Francis and I lived two kilometres away from the theatre, and we did not have a car. We woke up at half past four in the morning: Alice had to be fed, changed and dressed; we had to wash, have breakfast, and then push the pram all the way to the theatre where we left Alice in her cradle next to Grethe Pedersen, our secretary at the time, or Sigrid Post, who is still our accountant. We then changed rapidly into our training clothes and entered the space where the work started punctually at seven.

Alice was too young to go to the *dagmamma* during the first months, so it was the secretaries and assistant directors who took turns to care for her while I worked. The fact that I needed to breastfeed her involved a thirty-minute break every three hours. This interrupted Eugenio's creative flow since he was accustomed to working with us for hours on end without stopping. We finished working at around five or six in the afternoon, when we rushed to do shopping and went home to cook, wash Alice, feed her, play with her, wash the clothes and so on. We were very tired in the evenings and Alice's infant colic meant that we did not get a lot of rest at night. We worked six days a week, but only half-days on Saturdays.

When she was nine months old Alice started to go to the *dagmamma* from eight in the morning to four in the afternoon. To keep everyone on an equal footing, Eugenio decided that from then onwards the work would start at eight instead of seven. Eugenio himself continued to arrive at the theatre at seven o'clock.

Then there were the tours. What to do? I did not have a precedent to guide me. The only option was to resolve problems as they came along. Alice has had various nannies, all of whom were qualified nursery teachers from Holstebro. For the long tour in Latin America in 1987 we chose instead a nurse from Copenhagen who could speak Spanish. The organisers funded her travel and accommodation expenses, whilst Francis, Torgeir and I paid her salary and board.

Life is an improvisation.

We were in Mexico in 1987, presenting *The Gospel According to Oxyrhincus* in Monterrey.

In the hotel room the nanny was brushing her teeth, and lifting her eyes she saw in the mirror the reflection of Alice in her pyjamas sitting on the bed. Tears were falling silently down her little cheeks and she said wistfully: 'I miss Møborg'. Møborg is the name of a village twenty kilometres away from Holstebro where Torgeir, Francis and I had

Alice Carreri Pardeilhan (Bonn, 1984).

been living for four years with Alice. My heart broke when the nanny told me what had happened. Luckily we were in the final stage of our tour with *The Gospel According to Oxyrhincus*.

Two months later Francis moved to Italy and Alice began attending school. A new period was about to start for us. I would not be participating in the next group performance.

In 1990 Torgeir, Alice and I relocated to the centre of Holstebro. At this point it was possible for my mother to come over from Milan to take care of Alice during the periods when we were on tour. Eugenio had also been clever to improvise a rule that the new group performance would travel for only four months in any year. The other activities were held in Holstebro, and those that happened abroad did not require my presence. It was then, while thinking about creating new pedagogical initiatives in Holstebro while my companions were on tour with *Talabot*,[4] that I came up with the idea of Odin Week.

Like the creation of our performances, all the solutions were found along the way rather than beforehand.

To whoever is interested in knowing what happened to that child in pyjamas crying in a hotel room in Monterrey in 1987, I can say that she left Holstebro when she was nineteen and moved to Copenhagen where, after two years of ceramics schooling and two years at university studying humanities, she passed the entry requirements of the Rytmisk Musikkonservatorium (Academy of Rhythmic Music), from where she graduated in 2009. She dreams of a life singing jazz.

Notes

1 César Brie is an Argentinian actor who joined Odin Teatret in 1979 as a member of Iben Nagel Rasmussen's pedagogical project Farfa. He then participated in the group performances *Marriage with God*, *Talabot*, and *The Rooms in the Emperor's Palace*. He left Odin Teatret in 1988.
2 Kai Erik Bredholt, a Danish actor and musician, joined Odin Teatret in 1988. Since then he has participated in all group performances as well as in *Itsi Bitsi* (with Jan Ferslev and Iben Nagel Rasmussen).
3 Walter Ybema assisted in the direction of *Brecht's Ashes*.
4 *Talabot*, 1988–1991. A performance dedicated to Hans Martin Berg and Christian Ludvigsen. Actors: César Brie, Jan Ferslev, Richard Fowler, Naira Gonzalez, Falk Heinrich, Iben Nagel Rasmussen, Isabel Ubeda, Julia Varley and Torgeir Wethal. (Falk Heinrich and Isabel Ubeda replaced César Brie and Naira Gonzalez in 1990. It was really a second version of the performance which was then presented in the following year). Dramaturgy and direction: Eugenio Barba.

20 Marble

Every time we started work on a new performance Eugenio tried to put himself and us, his actors, in a new situation.

Working with the same actors and the same director for many years has advantages and disadvantages. The obvious advantage that comes about as a result of knowing one another is the deep reciprocal trust and the shared language of work that permits efficient communication. On the other hand, the disadvantage of working with the same core of persons over and over again involves the risk of monotony for both director and actors. When we start work on a new performance we feel compelled to invent strategies that surprise and stimulate us reciprocally.

The work on *The Gospel According to Oxyrhincus* began with the choice of costumes.

The space was divided in two by a black cloth. At the back, hidden from view, lay the treasure Eugenio had collected from his latest travels in Latin America with the new performance in mind. Standing next to the black cloth with a pack of cards in his hands, he invited all the actors to take a card. The one who picked the lowest card was the first to step behind the cloth and choose something for their costume. We then took turns going behind the cloth. When all of us had been behind the curtain, we went again in the same order to pick new elements until the treasure was exhausted and we had our arms full of fabric, costumes and accessories.

In my first visit behind the cloth I saw that there were all the dress elements of a Mãe de Santo.[1] Every time one of my colleagues emerged from behind the black curtain I was afraid they had selected a part of what I had immediately recognised as 'my' costume. But nobody did so.

In April 1974, at the beginning of the rehearsals of *Come! And the Day Will Be Ours* (which lasted two years), Eugenio told us that every actor would be given two characters: an explicit one and a secret one.

We were told not to disclose the identity of the secret character to anyone. Eugenio compared these two characters to the two horses used in battle by warriors of a tribe who fought against Alexander the Great. The warrior would utilise the two horses to conceal himself in the course of a battle, to bounce from one to the other with the aim of confusing the enemy, and to have at least one with which to return to camp. The secret character helps the actor to jump between two identities, thus avoiding the risk of giving a two-dimensional image of the explicit character. A strategy, therefore, aimed at avoiding the pitfall of clichés. If an actor does not manage to give shape to their explicit character, they can always fall back on the secret one for inspiration.

My explicit character for *The Gospel According to Oxyrhincus* was Antigone, and my secret character was Tereza Batista Tired of War, the protagonist of Jorge Amado's novel *Tereza Batista: Home from the Wars*.

Antigone's costume of a Mãe de Santo – with its numerous layers of wide white skirts rustling around my bare legs – influenced my interpretation of physical scores. To me it conveyed a way of movement that evoked the sacredness and sensuality characteristic of warm climates. On the smooth wooden catwalk at the centre of the set of *The Gospel According to Oxyrhincus*, I worked barefoot once again.

The Gospel According to Oxyrhincus was the first performance not to be based on actors' improvisations but rather on what Eugenio called 'marble' – that is, a series of physical actions created by two actors who worked together with the same object. The name 'marble' derived from the fact that these physical scores did not have the kind of personal roots typical of individual improvisations, but were raw material to be elaborated and 'sculpted'.

For example, a colleague and I lifted a chair by holding its legs with both of our hands. Whenever I lifted my right hand and lowered the left, the change in the chair's position compelled my colleague to react with his arms and torso. Similarly, whenever my colleague moved the 'flying' chair around, I was forced to comply with his intention and change my position in the space. The weight of the object helped us to execute actions with all of our bodies.

We could use any object: a plastic tube, a piece of cloth, a rope. The sequence of actions did not correspond to an imaginary content. The object was used to execute physical actions such as pushing, pulling and lifting. For example, the piece of cloth could be wrapped around a companion's shoulders, but it could not be used as a shawl for protection against the cold or as a flag. Rather, the cloth could be used to get the companion to lower down or to draw her towards you.

Once memorised, these sequences were repeated without the object: first in pairs and then individually. The actor then had to adapt them to one's own character and to the relations with the other characters in the scene. Therefore, the actor had to fill them up with meaning.

It was at this point that the term 'material' entered our work vocabulary to indicate all the fixed scores created, in various ways, for a performance.

At one point during the rehearsals Eugenio needed some new material. Since I had already used up my 'marble' we decided to do an improvisation, and we set up the video camera in the black room to record it. I wore my costume but I do not remember why. Eugenio gave me a theme. It did not resonate in me. The work at that period was very intense, added to which there was Alice, who was very young and who woke up frequently during the night. All the tiredness that had been accumulating had finally caught up with me. It was like sleeping while awake. Not a single image or idea came to mind. Just then, I remembered a nursery rhyme I read to Alice every night. I started to think this text, word by word, as I embodied the images by means of actions.

The fact that I was wearing my costume led me to perform actions with the physical dynamics of my character, a Brazilian Candomblé 'holy woman'. In this magical world I changed the size of objects: I stirred the soup with a spoon as big as an oar, I spread the tablecloth on a table as small as a book, and so on.

I had ignored the theme which Eugenio gave me, but the sequence of actions I created from the nursery rhyme was easy to memorise because I had a thread to follow.

Even today, after so many years, I use texts that I know well as a point of departure to rapidly develop and memorise an improvisation. The poem 'San Martino' by Giosuè Carducci, which I had learnt in childhood, is an example. Here is a rough translation of the opening lines: 'Towards the rugged hills, the drizzling mist ascends, and beneath the northwest wind howls and foams the sea ...' One of the first images we encounter in the poem is mist; I begin by touching a wall of mist in front of me, and then slowly my sight becomes misty until I myself become mist. I move in the space and I am struck by the thought of my cousin's death: the car he was driving on a motorway crashed suddenly into another due to dense fog. Now I am the car that runs and crashes. I fall, dead.

I can look at the mist, I can be the mist, or I can even freely associate about mist. In this way, even a brief text can serve as Ariadne's thread for a relatively long improvisation.

I can be the hunter who picks up a dead bird and in the next instant I can be the dead bird which is picked up by the hunter.

Through my training I have acquired the psychophysical capacity to alternate between the subject and object of an action.

Note

1 Pai de Santo and Mãe de Santo are the highest spiritual authorities of Candomblé, the African religion brought over to Brazil by slaves. They are the high priests responsible for the religious ceremonies that take place in the *terreiro*.

21 Meeting the Asian masters

The first session of ISTA was held in Bonn in 1980. It lasted a month but I was only there for fifteen days. Eugenio thought of inserting the lion dance[1] in *The Million* and so he asked Katsuko Azuma, a master of Nihon Buyo, to teach it to me.

Working with Katsuko Azuma on the basic positions of the Japanese classical dance was a decisive experience in my professional development.

Until then, in my training I had focused my attention towards the 'external' body: the limbs, the torso and the head. Katsuko taught me something else. She told me to imagine a steel ball covered in velvet in my stomach and a steel cable stretched out between the top of my head and my coccyx. This cable was tightly drawn, in tension, pulled upwards by the head towards the sky and downwards by the coccyx towards the centre of the earth. That is how she taught me to perform the basic positions of Nihon Buyo. It seems contradictory to speak of 'performing' a position, but this position is not static at all – it is dynamic in its apparent immobility.

I had to learn to feel my body from within and to embody the tensions that Katsuko told me about. These are micro-tensions that I later called *in-tensions*. *In-tensions* do not have anything to do with that tension which sometimes takes hold of parts of the actor's body when they stiffen up due to insecurity – for example, a hand, the nape of the neck, the ankles, or one's brows.

Katsuko's directions were not always easy to put into practice. Luckily, however, years of training had taught me how to learn.

In addition to Katsuko's lessons, I also attended the daily demonstrations of Balinese and Peking Opera masters, and every afternoon I met with Sanjukta Panigrahi for an hour to learn the basic positions of Odissi dance.[2] In teaching me the *tribhangi*,[3] Sanjukta compelled me first of all to break my daily habits of thinking about the lines of the body and to create a new balance according to the lines of tension she indicated.

Meeting the Asian masters 103

From *ISTA Dance*: a jump inspired by the Japanese classical dance Nihon Buyo.

From *ISTA Dance*: basic positions of Nihon Buyo.

When news of Sanjukta's death reached me in 1997, I was on holiday at home. It was a beautiful Danish summer day. The first thing that came to my mind was: without her the world is a poorer place. Sanjukta Panigrahi had become the queen of ISTA. For years her Odissi dances had lit up the scene of Theatrum Mundi and filled the spectators' hearts with strength and beauty.[4] What Sanjukta taught me by example was to believe in the need to do one's work and to accept its consequences.

In the work of the Balinese actors I was particularly attracted by their tendency to amplify every movement. They were wonderfully extreme in the way they raised their shoulders up to their ears, walked with their knees bent at right angles and lit up their eyes. The energy of their eyes was, perhaps, what fascinated me most about them.

In addition to rehearsing the lion dance, after my experience at the Bonn ISTA I continued to practise the basic principles of Balinese, Indian and Chinese dances, seeking to recreate the specific internal tensions of each dance. It was on the basis of this training that I created what I called *ISTA Dance*, which I now use at the beginning of *Traces in the Snow*.

From *ISTA Dance*: positions inspired by the Indian Odissi dance.

Thinking in terms of 'changes of energy' or the 'logic of tensions' opened new possibilities for me; it was a very fertile period in my training.

Later on, when Odin Teatret was invited to the Jerusalem International Festival in 1984, I saw a Butoh dance performance for the first time. I was captivated.[5] The assertion that attraction is the first step towards knowledge once again proved to be true. What struck me about the work of Natsu Nakajima and her collaborator was the extreme slowness and intensity of their movement. Instead of boring me, this extraordinary slowness, imbued with energy, served to awaken my senses. Thanks to Eugenio's intervention, it was possible for me to participate in a workshop that Natsu was giving at the time, even though it had already started. Her training was fast and violent, with elements from martial arts. I could not recognise any of the slowness I had perceived in her performance, and this increased my interest.

In 1986 I decided to go to Tokyo to work with Natsu during the summer holidays.

From *ISTA Dance*: positions inspired by Balinese dance.

Each day we began with two hours of very intense physical work that contained elements of Japanese police training; these were then followed by another two hours of improvisation. In the latter part we used the basic position of Noh theatre: the spine was infused with a tension that began from the top of the head, which we imagined to be stretched towards the sky, while the coccyx was drawn to the earth, exactly like the basic position of Nihon Buyo that I had learnt from Katsuko Azuma. Then we melted this position creating choreographies of extreme slowness fixed by Natsu with an apprentice who, in turn, transmitted them to me.

One of the choreographies was based on images from Jean Clos's sculptures. Natsu made me repeat it, changing the quality of energy from one image to another – for example, alternating the energy of stone with that of running water or of mist. She made me improvise the same choreography with three different types of music. After five weeks she chose one and gave it to me on a cassette, saying, 'This is your music'.

I had never shared the same choreography (or 'score', according to Odin Teatret vocabulary) with anyone before then. I was surprised

by the fact that the same choreography, performed by two different persons to different pieces of music, could evoke such diverse associations and look so dissimilar as to make it appear as if it were two separate entities.

For me, the most remarkable aspect of this apprenticeship was the work with the eyes. The basic task was to relax the eye muscles as much as possible until one's vision was completely blurred. 'You no longer see what is in front of you, you do not want to see it, it does not interest you. It does not matter what your eyes do, as long as you try to see inside you. Do not direct your gaze to the outside, but to the inside,' Natsu repeated.

At the beginning she would make me repeat the sequence based on Jean Clos's sculptures, beating the rhythm with a tambourine in order to make me understand how long I should keep each image. The precision that Natsu demanded went beyond the physical precision that Eugenio expected of me during rehearsals. Natsu's was a mental precision that left an ample margin for physically improvisation and allowed me to explore my score each time as if it were the first time.

In the same period I attended three evening classes a week with Kazuo Ohno in his Yokohama studio.[6] His instructions were very evocative. He used to say, 'For you, in the West, dance is what you see the body doing, but the true dance is what happens inside the dancer's body.'

From *ISTA Dance*: positions inspired by Butoh dance.

In the first evening, Kazuo Ohno asked us to explore, through movement on the spot, contact with our *kokoro*, a term which in Japanese refers to the soul-heart (that is, the 'heart' as the seat and source of feelings). In the second evening we tried to find the *kokoro* while walking and in *ma*: that is, in moments of immobility in which even breathing is blocked but where the mind continues to project itself in action.

Kazuo Ohno also insisted on the importance of the eyes. He said, 'Your eyes have to be holes, they should not see anything. They should be like the eyes of the dead that see everything and see nothing. When the eyes do not see, they allow the *kokoro* to shine through – that is, the centre, the soul-heart.'

In the process that I had to undergo to find this quality of the eyes, the world around me became blurred; I stopped seeing it and it lost its importance, and I lost my sense of time. On the other hand, the images from my choreography dilated to occupy my entire mind. I did not see what was around me and this, paradoxical though it may seem, gave me a sense of great security. I stopped worrying about how I looked, and concentrated myself entirely on being present in the image that I was embodying.

My body became a bell jar inside of which I felt secure, and my *kokoro* could move freely without the body hiding its dance.

Until that moment, training as I had with my eyes focused outward, I always had a precise idea of how I looked. With the removal of that focus, the capacity to see myself from outside vanished. I remember how shocking it was for me to see, for the first time, photographs of my character in *Judith* because I did not have the faintest idea of how I looked.

Katsuko Azuma, Natsu Nakajima and Kazuo Ohno showed me a completely new way of feeling my body, not from the outside but from within. They made me discover what I now call the 'internal body', revealing parts of myself that were hidden even to me.

Notes

1 This refers to the spectacular Shishi dance where the Chinese mythological figure of the lion shakes its mane frenetically. See photographs of Katsuko Azuma's interpretation of the dance in Eugenio Barba and Nicola Savarese (eds), *The Secret Art of the Performer: A Dictionary of Theatre Anthropology*, 2nd ed. (London: Routledge, 2006), pp. 252–53.
2 Sanjukta Panigrahi was an Indian master of Odissi dance. She contributed substantially to the reconstruction and revival of the dance by conducting research work with other scholars on the codification of the dance based on

ancient manuscripts and temple sculptures from the region of Orissa. Her collaboration with Eugenio Barba began in 1977 when, together with other Indian masters, she gave a workshop (organised by Odin Teatret in Holstebro) on classical forms of Indian dance and theatre. Panigrahi was one of the founding members of ISTA and participated in the first ten sessions held between 1980 and 1996. She died in 1997.

3   *Tribhangi* literally means 'three arches' and refers to a basic position in Odissi dance in which the body bends in the form of an S that passes through the head, shoulders, hips and knees.

4   Theatrum Mundi refers to the performance, directed by Eugenio Barba, which is presented at the end of each ISTA session and on other occasions. The performance involves masters from various Asiatic and Western traditions who, along with Odin Teatret actors, make up the artistic staff of ISTA.

5   The performance was *The Garden* by the Butoh dance company Muteki-Sha, established in Tokyo in 1979 by Natsu Nakajima, a student and collaborator of Tatsumi Hijikata.

6   Born in Hokkaido in 1906, Kazuo Ohno is a Japanese dancer, choreographer and pedagogue. He founded Butoh dance with Tatsumi Hijikata, with whom he started to collaborate in 1954.

22 *Judith*

Odin Teatret's ensemble performances emerge from an idea or a need of Eugenio's. Work demonstrations and performances with one actor or two or three actors arise instead from the actors' needs, and they have deep roots in training.

When I went to Japan in 1986 to work with Natsu Nakajima I was in a period of personal crisis. Alice was starting school in Holstebro the following year and this would mean that I could not continue touring with the group. At the same time I longed to have a child with Torgeir, with whom I had been living for years, but I could not make up my mind whether to do so or not, and this filled me with anguish.

I left for Japan with a heavy heart and nostalgia for the child I did not have. Natsu Nakajima told me that in Butoh one dances one's joys and sorrows. She had just lost Tatsumi Hijikata, who had been her master and point of reference for more than twenty years. Now she wanted to dance his death. Natsu's only apprentice had also just lost her twin brother, who had killed himself, and she wanted to do a performance to dance his death. In this context it was natural for me to dance my painful nostalgia. Not wanting to disclose all the details, I told Natsu about the theme I chose: a woman expecting a child. We called the woman Mary because Natsu immediately thought of the mother of Jesus. The theme of the choreography we composed together was, for me, that of the 'unborn prince', while for Natsu it was Mary's story.

Our work gave rise to a series of fixed scores that I showed Eugenio and the other Odin actors on my return from Japan. Some months later Eugenio offered to create a performance based on this material. A solo performance would allow me to balance my work as an actress with my needs as a mother. Eugenio gave me some tasks and the catalogue of an exhibition held in Florence in 1986: *The Magdalene Between the Sacred and the Profane*. After Jesus's death Mary Magdalene escaped from Jerusalem, perhaps with child. There it was again – my theme of the 'unborn prince'. I studied the images in that book and discovered that despite the passing of centuries, some of them still had a strong evocative power. I photocopied some of the images and placed them next to each other on the floor, and then began to reproduce the different poses with my body.

As the tour with *The Gospel According to Oxyrhincus* proceeded, I continued to develop the tasks set by Eugenio. I travelled with a foldable deckchair and a portable stereo that I used during my daily training. In the morning, in the same space in which we were performing that evening, I physically memorised the images I had chosen from the exhibition catalogue and used them to create sequences of actions that I would adapt to various pieces of music and in which I would work with different objects. In this way I elaborated a number of sequences of images: Mary Magdalene carrying the scented oil; as she bathed Jesus's feet; beneath the cross; in ecstasy.

Afterwards I tried to find a rhythm to link the various images in a flow. I chose a song, but so as not to 'spread butter on lard' (as we say in Denmark), I did not opt for a dramatic piece: the images were already so. At first I used a lullaby, but this was known only in Italy. Eventually I chose a song that also evoked the image of a child in other countries: the Christmas carol *Silent Night*.

In the meantime, I continued to explore some principles from Butoh during my training. Namely, I explored the idea that the dancer does not represent a character but its ghost, or shadow, and that one works with elements taken from nature. For example, Natsu told me to repeat choreographies more than once, each time giving me different directions: 'You are stone. You are mist. Earth. Water. Air.'

In July 1987, two days after the filming of *The Gospel According to Oxyrhincus*[1] had ended, Eugenio and I started rehearsing. I showed him the material I had accumulated, which included, as well as the training, the choreographies I had created with the Butoh masters in Japan and the result of the tasks that he had given me.

Eugenio imagined that in order to create a dramatic situation, I had to act in relation to another character. On the basis of my material, this person should be on the floor; perhaps we could have used only his head. So Eugenio thought of Salome. It seemed to me a very interesting proposition because in alternating between Mary Magdalene and Salome I had the possibility of oscillating between the sacred and the profane. Once again I found myself in dialogue with a secret character.

A sequence of actions based on images depicting Mary Magdalene.

Subsequently, he suggested that I explore the figure of Judith from the Old Testament. He had read various writings on the complex nature of her story. Judith can be seen as a holy woman who performs a ritual and acts under holy command, or as a cold and calculating woman who falls for Holofernes' charms and kills him because she cannot resist him. In these two interpretations the sacred and the profane met in the same character. I did not need to think of Mary Magdalene or Salome any longer because Judith included both.

Eugenio set to work to elaborate all the material in relation to the story of Judith. Then he asked me to prepare other material with some objects that he provided himself.

When I showed him the sequence of the Magdalene images accompanied by *Silent Night*, he suggested substituting the song with a love monologue which we created together from various fragments of different poems.

At Odin Teatret, we follow various routes before we reach the definitive text of a performance. Sometimes we start from a work by a single author, which we can then elaborate radically. At other times it is either Eugenio or one of the actors who writes the text. Often, the director and actors propose poems, novels and newspaper articles from which dialogues and monologues are extracted. At other times we choose the most evocative fragments from an author's entire work.

The text, just like the performance, emerges from the interaction between the director and the actors.

For *Judith*, I had gathered a number of poems by Paul Eluard. Eugenio had chosen Friedrich Hebbel's version of the story where Judith, a young Jewish widow who is rich, beautiful and childless, falls in love with the charismatic figure of the supreme commander of the Assyrian forces, Holofernes, before she kills him to save her people. In the performance I address the love poem to Holofernes' decapitated head. The physical score that I had originally created on the basis of the Magdalene images underwent changes so that it could be adapted to the new context.

Once, during our rehearsals, Eugenio asked me to show him a scene that I had with Tom Fjordefalk in *Come! And the Day Will Be Ours*. Then he told me to repeat it following the logic of Butoh dance. In this scene I took off Tom's Indian poncho, made him wear a white shirt and a pair of shoes, wrapped him up in a military blanket and placed a black hat on his head. How to perform the same sequence without him? After an initial moment of bewilderment, I remembered what Natsu had told me: 'In a scene you can alternate between being the subject and the object of an action.' In the case of my sequence with Tom, I was the one performing the actions while he was the object at the receiving end. To do the same thing in his absence I had to alternate between doing and receiving the actions. Apart from a change in the energy of my eyes, the immediate result was an increase in the intensity and a reduction of the speed in my actions.

This was how the work on the final scene of *Judith* began.

Judith was completed in a month of rehearsals. No performance before that time had been created so rapidly. A couple of days after its premiere in August 1987 Alice started school, and Eugenio and the others left for Fara Sabina to begin rehearsals on *Talabot*, the new ensemble performance which I was not taking part in.

During its first run, a performance is still in the process of taking shape. It needs at least fifty presentations before it stabilises and reaches its final form. For weeks, months and years Eugenio fights to instil life in it, first by protecting the actors' creativity in the initial period, and then by following his own logic to guide the spectator's sensorial voyage.

A performance is like an organism: it can only grow or die. It is the actors who make a performance grow. Knowing their scores perfectly, they can concentrate on what is essential on stage: to listen and react. This is the only condition that allows a performance to live and not become mere repetition.

I have been asked, more than once, how I continue to present the same performance – with fixed physical and vocal scores – for so many years.

I do not think that this question is asked with the same frequency to a musician who has played Chopin's *Nocturnes* or Bach's *Goldberg Variations* for years. For me, there is no difference between that musician and myself. The musician repeats a fixed score, written by someone else perhaps in a different age, but with time his interpretation gains in confidence, experience, phrasing and detail. It is no mystery: when one is confident of what one does, one is more open towards the world and can 'dance' with it. For me, the score is a means that allows my *kokoro* to make contact with the *kokoro* of other people. I use this Japanese term because 'centre' is too technical a word, and for me 'soul' is too loaded with religious overtones. In the Japanese term *kokoro* these two meanings merge and balance each other.

I have often been asked about how I prepare myself before a performance. Rather than *what* I do in these instances, it is more a question of *how* I do it.

I always arrive at the theatre a couple of hours before the performance starts; I iron the clothes, put the props in their place on stage, do some stretching exercises and warm up my voice. Putting on makeup, even ever so lightly, is the most important moment because, as Bertolt Brecht says in a beautiful poem,[2] it helps me to remove every personal trace from my face.

Silence is not absolute, but it prevails while I empty my mind of daily concerns. Emptiness is my point of departure.

In *Judith* I do not relate to other actors. I have to focus with all of my being to listen and react to my partners: my mental images and the music.

I began to perform *Judith* in 1987. Is the *Judith* of 2014 the same as that of 1987? Is the Roberta Carreri of 1987 the same person in 2014? Yes and no.

The performance is the same: I have not changed the soundtrack, the text or the sequence of actions, but I am different. A person changes and so does an actor, but what remains immutable is the significance of the moment on stage.

I have to inhabit every moment of the performance as if it were a large hall. I have to phrase every action, to perform it as if it were the only opportunity I have been given to do so, to live every performance as if it were the last. I should neither rush through nor linger over my actions.

Flow appears only when fear disappears, and fear disappears with exercise. That is why training and a long rehearsal period are necessary.

I see someone flying a hand-glider: they fly when their thought becomes action.

I see two strangers dancing the tango: the dance occurs when they cease to think about what they have to do and let their bodies react to the knowledge they have acquired over the years. The body that knows, does not think, reacts.

To go beyond technique, I need to do away with the thought/action, mind/body dichotomy.

The greatest flautist *is* the music he plays. The greatest singer *is* the song she sings. The greatest actor *is* the action she performs. In front of them, also the spectator, forgetting himself, becomes part of the sound, the dance, the action.

There isn't a greater silence than the one in front of two hundred spectators during a performance. There is a moment in *Traces in the Snow* when this silence occurs every time. It is a magical moment. The privilege of reliving it is probably one of the reasons why I do theatre.

Notes

1 *In the Beginning was the Idea*, directed by Torgeir Wethal (Odin Teatret Film, 1991).
2 'My face is made up, purified from / every personality, made empty, to reflect / the thoughts, from now on more than ever, changing like / the voice and gesture', 'Trucco' (Make Up), in *Bertolt Brecht: Poesie 1913–1956* (Turin: Einaudi 1977), p. 387 (translated from Italian by Frank Camilleri).

23 Notes on improvisation

The rhythm of producing performances was markedly slow in the 1970s due to the time that actors took to memorise the improvisations which were recorded on film. In the early 1980s Torgeir invented a way of creating material that he called 'one step at a time'. An actor performs an action and then repeats it, performs a second action and repeats the first and the second, performs a third action and repeats the first, the second and the third. In this way an actor composes and memorises a series of actions at the same time.

I used this method to work on the improvisation theme that Eugenio gave us in May 1992 at the beginning of what eventually became the creation of *Kaosmos*. Eugenio regularly creates for us opportunities for research. They are privileged moments during which we embark on a voyage without knowing the destination, and in which we always discover something that we were not expecting. It is a way of reflecting on our profession as well as reinforcing the unity of the group. The theme for these meetings can be either the exploration of training or preparing the ground for a new performance.

> *Thursday 7 May 1992*
> *We enter the black room dressed elegantly, carrying with us a blanket or something of the sort. I had a Peruvian poncho. I'm dressed in black, in a light dress and a tight-fitting little coat, and wearing high-heeled shoes.*
>
> *Some months ago Eugenio gave us the task to read Rudyard Kipling's* The Jungle Book *for today.*
>
> *He began by giving us the collective theme of improvisation.*
>
> *'How is a wolf born?' he asks, and then continues: 'There are three ways: the literal-biological one (the cub, in its mother's belly with its siblings, begins the journey towards the earth, where there is light and darkness); the action that sees a young person move from anonymity to the ranks of those who have a name (an initiation rite that lasts eleven nights*

with ablutions, walking on embers, rolling in brambles, becoming accustomed to venom ...); the one that occurs when one is old, the third birth, when one has outgrown early youth and people say: he/she is a true wolf. The quality of the wolf has developed.

'We'll work on these three births. Take a little "flying carpet", which is enough for one person. Put it on the floor and let it become your personal macrocosm. The carpet becomes the jungle. The she-wolf gives birth on the carpet. The old man sits on the carpet to see the ritual that allows the youth to find his "I". Put the carpet in the right place. Go through the three births and memorise them. In the carpet you are weaving, you have to find knots that have the possibility of being verbalised. Every birth has to have its own knots, which are many and have words. For example, in the first birth: dawn, effort, twilight. The third birth is in the third person: "He is righteous." Humility is perceived from the outside.

'Khipu means "thread of knots" and was the name of Incan writing.

'Every knot that you create has to have the character of a swollen corpse on the side of the road: it is dead but full of life, full of shrewdness. Find words that help you to transform (yourself).

'When you are ready, sit down and watch what your colleagues are doing. Then write the Khipu – that is, "words in freedom". What characterises the poem (something done by the poet = the one who does) is that the words are chosen. The poet frees words from their univocal meaning and gives them the freedom to mean much more. Words become "action". Then give me a copy of your Khipu.'

In my work diary I give a step-by-step description of my improvisation on the limited space of a Peruvian poncho. Here are the notes that remind me of the improvisation I made following the theme proposed by Eugenio:

First birth. *I lie down with my left hip on my poncho. My left leg is in a foetal position. My left arm is partly stretched out. My right leg is stretched forward. My right arm is spread out with the hand on the floor close to my face. I am Mother Earth: half foetus, half midwife. I push with my right hand on the floor and then lift my forefinger like a sprouting bud. When my arm is stretched upwards, I open and close my hand. I grasp the light and bring it towards me. I open towards the right. I am a wolf cub, I touch my little siblings with my right elbow. I open my hand and with my fingers touch the muzzle of a third sibling and the chin of a fourth. I caress the fifth above my head. Then they all start to push me from the back.*

I become the she-wolf (with my face on the floor, lying down on my heels). I push forward with my right hand and left elbow on the floor. I push three times.

I become the wolf cub. I rise and sit on my heels. All the time my eyes are closed. I spit a necklace of coral. I scratch my belly, smilingly. I lift my right hand and then my left hand to my nose. I sniff in both directions. I hold the she-wolf's teats between my fingers. I smile. A sibling (my right hand) bites my right ear. With my left hand I hit him with a paw and get rid of him. I make room with my shoulders and elbows, and half-open my eyes that are brimming with water.

I grow like a tree, in every direction. Then I relax, taking a step backwards.

Second birth. *'Sun dance' (arched). I draw a semi-circle tapping my feet. I stop on the 'holy place' and begin to swing. I sway through the jungle. I regain my balance by adjusting my spine. I turn. I look at the burning coal. I cover my nose with my right hand and use my left hand as blinkers. I walk forward using my arms. I reach the end of the jungle and begin to explore its boundaries, passing through brambles. When I reach the 'holy place', I kneel and sit with my legs to one side. I place my hands in the form of a cross on the 'holy place' and begin to gather berries with my left forefinger, which I then put on my lower lip. On the fourth berry, I let my finger slide down my stomach and the fire spreads there. Squat dance. When the dance ends, my eyes are closed. I am blind. There is 'fire' in my eyes behind closed eyelids. I kneel and indicate three points, and then I stand up. I catch a butterfly flying in front of me and bring it before my eyes. I touch the base of my nose and let the fingers slide down to my chin. I gently throw away the butterfly in front of me and open my eyes when it touches the floor.*

Third birth. *I have regained my sight. I turn my head and shoulders to the right while keeping the eyes and hips facing in front of me. I take a half-step forward and then retreat very slowly to the border of the jungle (the edge of the poncho). I lift my right fist to my right temple and leave my left arm swinging. My head sways a bit as well. Then I tap the floor silently with my right foot. A crescendo of movements with eyes closed. When the dance ends, I stroke my right cheek with my right fist. My face stiffens, the edges of my mouth droop, and my eyes are partly closed. I am the Old Wolf. Slowly, I put my hands on my hips and walk in a circle. My feet come across the necklace I spat at the beginning and crush it. I keep walking in a circle, ending with my right hand on my right shoulder.*

This was my *Khipu*:

> *I am Mother Earth: half foetus, half midwife.*
> *I push the earth. I pierce the earth. I am born from within the earth.*
> *Like a tree I spread inside the earth while high up I seek the light, I grasp it, I make it mine.*
> *I have five siblings: two nest next to my elbow and three beside my hand. Together they press me towards the light, while they push the she-wolf to give birth.*
> *I am the first and the last among the others who are in their turn the first and the last.*
> *I am.*
> *Satisfied.*
> *In the light I slowly open my eyes, which are full of water. I spread out in the light performing the sun dance. The night makes me sway, swing.*
> *The embers glow in the darkness. The wind makes them shine and wafts the smell of burnt flesh to me.*
> *I explore the borders.*
> *I immerse myself into the brambles, and reach the place of the holy berries.*
> *The fourth berry lights up the fire in me, and allows me to see in darkness. With it comes the knowledge of pain, and with it maturity, and with it the sense of loss.*

For the first months I worked on the performance without knowing who my character was, who performed the actions I performed, who sang the songs I sang. Whenever he had the opportunity, Eugenio would tell me: 'What you are doing is too much Judith'. Performing the same character for a number of years served to root its physical dynamic in me like a second nature, which risked influencing everything I did on stage.

Eugenio was still not sure about the identity of my character, but after insisting with him he agreed to tell me at least the name of my secret character: Medea.

Many months later, Eugenio decided that my character was the Mother from Hans Christian Andersen's 'The Story of a Mother'. To get away from the lightness of Judith, I chose to dress up my character in a heavy costume with various layers: to wrap my hair in an enormous woollen skein that wreathed my head, to wear heeled shoes and lots of jewellery.

Kaosmos gave us the opportunity to explore various possibilities of interpreting the score, both during and after the performance's lifetime.

In 1997 Isabel Ubeda[1] and Tina Nielson left the group, while Tage Larsen returned. *Kaosmos* thus came to an end and Eugenio organised the funeral of the performance. He opted to run the performance without the set, objects and costumes. He told us to wear whatever we wanted and to go to the white room. Two long tables – set up with bread, olives and wine – were placed on both sides of the space. The other diners consisted of friends who were invited for the 'funeral banquet' and who were seated behind a row of candles that illuminated the tables.

I left my hair loose, wore a cyclamen dress with white embroidery, and put on a pair of military shoes with leather soles. It was extraordinary how these shoes took possession of my character's scores in *Kaosmos* and transformed them completely, filling them with an unexpected vitality. A new character was born from a simple change in costume.

We showed the performance twice in succession: first with Tina and Isabel, and then, immediately after, with Tage, who had the task of using the entire duration of the performance to cross slowly from one end of the stage to the other.

Eugenio gave Tage a wooden board with which to improvise. He also inserted some texts from *The Gospel According to Oxyrhincus*, which could now be understood since they were not translated into Coptic. Eugenio called the second version of this performance *Inside the Skeleton of the Whale.*[2]

From the ashes of *Kaosmos* emerged also *Ode to Progress*.[3]

Eugenio asked us to turn our scores from *Kaosmos* into dances and then have them performed by our characters from *Anabasis* (our street theatre performance). In this way, Geronimo took over the dances of my scores. The structure of *Ode to Progress* did not provide enough space for all my *Kaosmos* scores. Therefore, when I was off stage I used some of my scores to react, seated or standing, to my companions' dances.

The same score can be 'assimilated', or rather performed, in a much reduced scale; if in *Kaosmos* I lifted my arm above my head, now I only lifted my forefinger with my hand still resting on my legs. Alternatively, I could perform my score in its entirety with only one part of my body – the eyes, for example, or the legs – but always sitting down. In every instance, however, I had to justify everything that I did in relation to the dances of my companions, deciding whether I was 'in favour' or 'against' what was happening.

Notes on improvisation 123

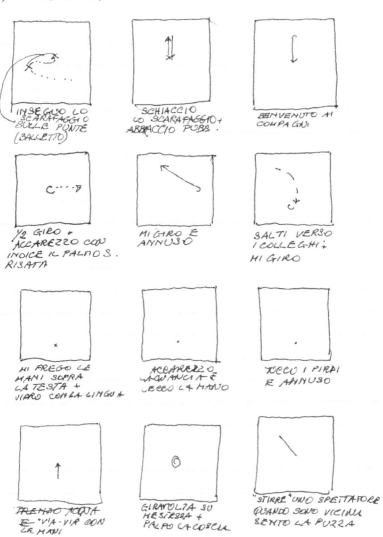

Annotations from my work diary detailing Geronimo's dance based on my *Kaosmos* scores.[4]

124 *The story and the training*

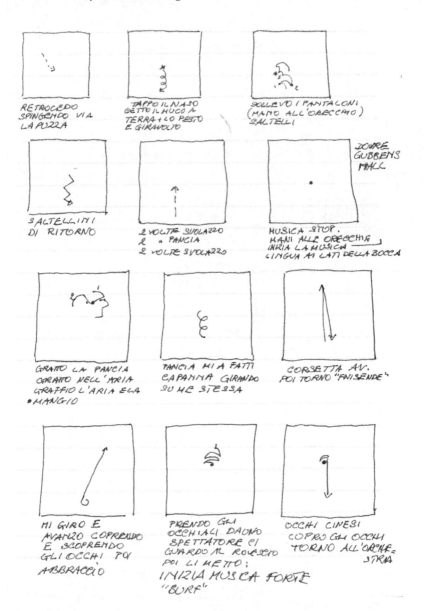

Notes on improvisation

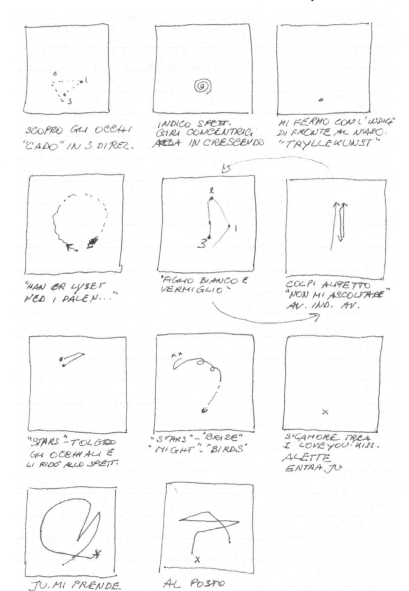

Following the logical thread of my score helped me to stay focused and kept my body-mind in dialogue with what was happening around me. In other words, I made sure that I was present on stage.

I often have the impression that actors believe that their thoughts are made invisible by the thickness of their skull. They are mistaken. The actor's body is transparent on stage: if the actor's mind is empty, the spectators will not see anything, but if the actor is mentally engaged, spectators will perceive this clearly and their minds will 'dance' with the actor's.

After all, this is the actor's task: to make the spectators' minds dance with them.

Notes

1 Isabel Ubeda, a Spanish actress of Odin Teatret from 1990 to 1997. She took part in the group performances of *Talabot*, *Rooms in the Emperor's Palace* and *Kaosmos*.
2 *Inside the Skeleton of the Whale*, 1997–present. Actors: Kai Bredholt, Roberta Carreri, Jan Ferslev, Tage Larsen, Iben Nagel Rasmussen, Julia Varley, Torgeir Wethal and Frans Winther. Dramaturgy and direction by Eugenio Barba.
3 *Ode to Progress*, first version 1997, second version 2003–present. A performance dedicated to Malika Boussof and Susan Sontag. Actors: Kai Bredholt, Roberta Carreri, Jan Ferslev, Tage Larsen, Iben Nagel Rasmussen, Julia Varley, Torgeir Wethal (until 2010) and Frans Winther. The second version also included the actor Augusto Omolú (until 2013). Dramaturgy and direction by Eugenio Barba.
4 The notes concern the first dance of Geronimo, including movement direction in space, encounters with fellow actors, acrobatic leaps, other physical actions, and coordination with music.

24 The voice in training and in performance

When I joined Odin Teatret, the vocal training of the actors was based on what Eugenio had learnt at Jerzy Grotowski's Teatr-Laboratorium.

The actors spoke the text using various resonators: occipital (back of the skull), head, mask, chest and abdomen.[1] Imagining the emission of sound from these parts of the body gave different colours to the sound of their voices.

We had to know the text we used in training so well that we did not need to make any effort to remember it. We did not follow the punctuation and we did not interpret the text. We spoke, and whenever we needed to breathe we inhaled, just like what happens in daily life.

During my first years at Odin Teatret Eugenio led my vocal training almost daily, without ever mentioning breathing techniques.

In the summer of 1974, in Carpignano Salentino, we did vocal training in the tobacco fields or on the seashore. Wide horizons opened in front of us. The first direction I remember receiving was to say a text and sing a song at the top of my voice.

It was the first time since my childhood, when I had been told I was tone deaf, that I sang so loudly.

Eugenio told me to project my voice towards the rising sun, the birds in the sky, the people who could be hiding behind the tamarisk trees, or to follow the rhythm of the waves in the sea and of the fronds of the trees as they moved in the wind.

On our return to Denmark in October, the vocal training was held indoors in our spaces. The horizons were now brought closer and the sonority of our voices changed.

To teach me how to find resonators, Eugenio made me speak to his hand.

To help me find the mask resonator, he told me to speak to his hand which he held two centimetres away from my lips. Then, moving it progressively further away, he asked me to increase the volume of my voice proportionately, making sure that I kept using the same resonator. It was difficult because when one increases the volume one intuitively tends to slide to a higher resonator. When Eugenio brought his hand gradually closer to my mouth I lowered the volume of my voice, and so I had to pay attention so as not to shift to a lower resonator. Then he moved his hand to other parts of my body – chest, abdomen, head and nape of the neck – telling me to use the corresponding resonator. The vocal action was always to follow his hand that moved more or less quickly, changing height and distance.

Another exercise that involved the use of different resonators consisted in improvising, supporting with the voice, an imaginary ball floating in the air. For example, I used the head resonator if the ball was on top of my head, the belly (the lowest resonator I could find) if it was at my feet, high volume if it was far away, low volume if it was nearby.

Sometimes Eugenio would tell me to address the text to various objects in the room which could be found at different distances and heights.

Eugenio made us work in couples to help us get accustomed to the effects of our vocal actions. Actor A stood with her back to actor B. Speaking a text she used in her daily vocal training, B had to guide the body of A in the space.[2] The vocal action consisted of moving a colleague away from or nearer to oneself. Then we swapped places so that both of us could learn how to guide a colleague in a precise way, turning a sound impulse into a physical reaction.

In addition to the five basic resonators we also used those of the nose and the throat, both of which could be combined with other resonators: head, mask and chest.

Eugenio told me to imitate Louis Armstrong or a lioness to help me find my throat resonator. For the nasal resonator he used the image of a pedantic professor.

Another principle that I used in vocal training was to 'colour' the voice, associating it with natural elements. For example, I would sing a song or say a text as if my voice was mist, fire or a stormy sea.

In the early years I often did vocal improvisations that, like the physical ones, started from a theme suggested by Eugenio. The task was to 'depict' through vocal actions the images that the theme aroused in me. The aim was to stop me from thinking in a technical way, allowing me to be carried away by the images, and in this way find new vocal sonorities. A possible theme could be 'Istanbul's bazaar', where one can find everything: hawkers, young people, old people, children, women, thieves, and people who sing, laugh or cry. There might also be dogs, cats, birds and mice. The images would determine the quality of my voice and I would reproduce them, letting my imagination go.

For me, an important aspect of both vocal and physical training is the alternation between moments of great technical rigour and moments of play.

For vocal improvisations we often used *volapyk* (which in Danish means a made-up language or incomprehensible jargon) that could contain sounds reminiscent of existing languages such as Russian, Finnish or Chinese.

In *volapyk*, as in the *grammelot* used by Commedia dell'Arte performers, the words do not mean anything at all, but through the sonority, melody and intensity of the voice they evoke associations in the minds of their hearers.

The important thing is to perform vocal actions in a precise way that allows their hidden sense to be picked up, even if one does not understand the meaning of the words.

It is a known fact that ninety percent of communication is non-verbal. The tone or melody with which one says a phrase can transmit the opposite message of the semantic meaning of the words. In life this is not a rare occurrence.

When Odin Teatret left Norway, it lost its common language shared by actors and spectators. Work on the evocative power of the voice thus became even more necessary. Danish is a different language than Norwegian and the actors who followed Eugenio in Denmark could not rid themselves of their strong accent. Eugenio opted not to make them use Danish on stage. Better still, he made the Danish actors speak Norwegian in *Kaspariana*[3] and *Ferai*.[4] However, even this was not a satisfactory option because they too had an accent when speaking in a foreign language.

From the 1970s onwards, various actors from different nationalities joined Odin Teatret. Each time Eugenio launched the work on a new performance, he tried to find a solution to the problem caused by the lack of a common language between the actors and also with the audience.

In the first performance, *Ornitofilene*, the actors spoke Norwegian, while in the second, *Kaspariana*, and the third, *Ferai*, they spoke different Scandinavian languages.

In *Min Fars Hus*, Eugenio opted for a *volapyk* that sounded like Russian.

In *Come! And the Day Will be Ours*, the actors spoke in English, Sioux, Cheyenne, Quiché and Ojibwe.

In *Brecht's Ashes*, Eugenio decided that Mack the Knife (Tage Larsen) would translate the German lines of Bertolt Brecht (Torgeir Wethal) into the language of the place where the performance was being presented. Every time we travelled to a new country we needed at least a week of rehearsals.

To avoid this problem, in the following performance, *The Gospel According to Oxyrhincus*, Eugenio translated all the texts, which he had chosen with great care, into Coptic and *koiné* Greek: two dead languages that were spoken in Egypt in the area where the Gnostic gospel scrolls were discovered. In this way spectators from all countries shared the fact that nobody could understand the semantic meaning of our words. However, the programme for the performance contained a translation of all the texts into the language of the audience where we were performing.

On the other hand, in *Kaosmos*, Eugenio had every actor speak in their native tongue. So we had a performance with Spanish, English, Italian, Danish and Norwegian, with only fragments of some texts being translated into the language of the place.

Since the ensemble was predominantly Danish and the performance was based on the texts of the Danish poet Henrik Nordbrandt, Danish was the language most used in the performance *Mythos*, though I continued to speak mainly in Italian and Julia in English. Initially Eugenio chose to translate all the text into five languages: Danish, French, English, Spanish and Italian, according to the country we were visiting. However, after a year it became clear that these language changes were having a significant effect on the rhythm of the performance. Therefore he decided to translate only some excerpts that were indispensible to understand the essential elements in the dramaturgy. The same strategy was used in *Andersen's Dream*.[5]

Holstebro is a small city of only thirty-two thousand inhabitants, but it has a big library that has been lending not only books but also music records since the early seventies. In addition to the music collections of folk, pop, jazz, rock, classical, lyrical and chamber music as well as musicals, there was also a section dedicated to world music, about which I became curious. During my first years at Odin Teatret I fell under the spell of harmonies that did not belong to my culture. Later, when I participated in ISTA and heard the songs, sounds and melodies of Balinese, Chinese, Indian and Japanese musicians, this interest grew and deepened.

One day, a young doctor who was doing service as a conscientious objector at Odin Teatret got to know of my interest in the singing of other cultures. He told me that there is no anatomical difference between the larynx of a Chinese, African, Eskimo or Italian person: they are all the same. All the sounds that I heard were also hidden in me – I only had to find them. My vocal training became the space for this research. During my vocal training I listened to the records I borrowed from the library and imitated the voice of the singers. My intention was certainly not to become an expert in the vocal techniques of Peking Opera or Kabuki; I simply wanted to find those specific sounds in me so that I could extend my range of vocal possibilities.

In the early 1980s John Hardy told us of the existence of harmonics,[6] a singing technique of Tuvan shepherds in Georgia on the border with Mongolia. The voices of Tuva are called 'crystal voices', not so much because they sing high notes or in falsetto, but rather because they are capable of simultaneously producing another sound on top of their voices: the harmonic. The sound is like the one produced by running a wet fingertip around the edge of a crystal glass. Harmonics can be very strong, sometimes resembling the sound of a flute playing simultaneously with a human voice.

In 1997 Eugenio chose to use harmonics to create the soundscape of *Mythos*. He invited Altai Hangai (a group of Mongolian musicians he met in Amsterdam), as well as Tran Quang Hai[7] and Michael Vetter,[8] to Holstebro so that they could teach us their techniques of harmonics.

When we create performances at Odin Teatret we work with both physical and vocal actions. We might decide that vocal actions should follow the physical action, which in turn might follow the action described in the text.

For example, when in the first monologue of *Judith* I say: 'Nebuchadnezzar called Olofernes, highest general of his army, and said: "Go and occupy the territory of the rebels"', I let the vocal and physical actions run parallel to each other, following the one described in the text.

I say: 'Go', using the mask resonator, projecting the voice far away while indicating in front of me.

Then: 'And occupy'. 'Occupy' means asserting that this place belongs to me; so I say the words with my chest resonator, lowering the volume of my voice while pointing at the floor at my feet.

And still further: 'The territory of the rebels', delineating the limits of the territory with a circle I make with the melody of my voice, while tracing a circle in the air with my right forefinger.

Left: 'Go…'. Right: '… and occupy'.

I can also decide to 'colour' single words in a phrase with my voice. For example, when I say: '[Judith] took her widow's clothes off, washed her body with water and anointed herself with thick perfume', the word 'water' evokes in me the feeling of cold water that slides down my back. So I let this image 'colour' the way I say this word.

For 'thick perfume' I choose a deep and heavy voice, just like I imagine the perfume to be.

At another point I say: 'She dressed in garments of celebrations with necklaces and bracelets'. I imagine the bracelets to be made of silver and think of the Italian expression 'a silver laugh'. So when I say the word 'bracelets' I enfold it in a 'silver smile'.

I can decide to underline the most important word in a phrase by not saying it loudly. When Judith says: 'The elderly of Bethulia decided to resist for five more days and to surrender if by then the Lord had not shown mercy to their city', I pronounce what for me is the most important word, 'mercy', in a lower voice than the one I use for the other words, forcing spectators to make an effort to hear it more clearly.

I colour some of the words in the text to make them stand out from the rest and to break the monotony. If I had to colour every word, I would risk creating an infernal cacophony.

The voice in training and in performance 133

She 'washed her body with water…'

My objective is to construct a rhythm that contains phrasing – that is, variations of intensity, speed and volume – in order to give a dynamic quality to the text.

'Phrasing' is an essential word in the world of music as much as it is in the work on text and actions.

Notes

1 See Jerzy Grotowski, *Towards a Poor Theatre* (London: Methuen, 1975), pp. 121–23. See also Raymonde Temkine, *Grotowski* (Avon: Discus, 1972), pp. 108–09, and Eugenio Barba, *Alla ricerca del teatro perduto* (Padova: Marsilio, 1965), pp. 143–45.
2 All this is documented in the film *Vocal Training at Odin Teatret*, directed by Torgeir Wethal (Odin Teatret Film, 1972), which was produced in collaboration with the Italian public broadcasting corporation RAI. The transcript of Eugenio Barba's commentary in the film can be found in Eugenio Barba, *Theatre – Solitude, Craft, Revolt* (Aberystwyth: Black Mountain Press, 1999), pp. 74–76.
3 *Kaspariana*, 1966–68. Actors: Jan Erik Bergström, Anna-Trine Grimnes, Lars Göran Kjellstedt, Else Marie Laukvik, Iben Nagel Rasmussen, Dan Nielsen and Torgeir Wethal. Text by Ole Sarvig. Adaptation and direction by Eugenio Barba.
4 *Ferai*, 1969–70. Actors: Ulla Alasjärvi, Marisa Gilberti, Juha Häkkänen, Sören Larsson, Else Marie Laukvik, Iben Nagel Rasmussen, Carita Rindell and Torgeir Wethal. Text by Peter Seeberg. Adaptation and direction by Eugenio Barba.
5 *Andersen's Dream*, 2004–11. A performance dedicated to Torzov and Dottor Dappertutto. Actors: Kai Bredholt, Roberta Carreri, Jan Ferslev, Elena Floris (2010–11), Mia Thiel Have (2004–06), Donald Kitt, Tage Larsen, Augusto Omolú, Iben Nagel Rasmussen, Julia Varley, Torgeir Wethal and Frans Winther. Dramaturgy and direction by Eugenio Barba.
6 John Hardy was a musician, composer and actor of Cardiff Laboratory Theatre.
7 Tran Quang Hai is a Vietnamese musician who, since the 1970s, has researched the technique of *khoomeilakh* (overtone singing) to become a world famous expert in this peculiar split-tone singing which is well known in Tuva and Mongolia.
8 Michael Vetter is a self-taught German musician who, since the 1970s, has been involved in the development of various vocal expressive possibilities, including research on 'intuitive music' and the 'music of language'. He then went on to specialise in the technical use of harmonics to compose *Oratorio Armonicale*, which has been performed in many churches in Europe.

25 *Salt*[1]

After the creation of *The Whispering Winds in Theatre and Dance*,[2] a demonstration in which I collaborated with Jan Ferslev[3] and which was presented at the Copenhagen ISTA in 1996, both Jan and I wanted to pursue the story of the character that had emerged in the process: a woman with a bundle who embarks on a voyage. The exploration of this theme, which became our form of training for five years, had nothing to do with the physical exercises of the early years. Now I was in the fourth season of my training.

In between tours, Jan and I went to the white room, and while he learnt how to play new musical instruments like the harp or the bagpipes, the mandolin or the water harp, I did exercises to warm up my body. Then, while Jan composed melodies as he improvised on the instruments, I created dances and action sequences based on his notes. In the evening I would scour through my library searching for reproductions of paintings to create various series of images which I could then link through sequences of actions. Starting from the theme of nostalgia, I found some texts by Fernando Pessoa and by Jeanette Winterson. I began to say the texts while performing the physical scores and the dances inspired by Jan's music.

During our tours abroad Jan bought a number of peculiar instruments and I acquired objects that, to my eyes, oozed with nostalgia: a small cardboard suitcase and a male celluloid doll, an old wrought iron garden chair, a small cut glass crystal bottle, a Portuguese coffee-pot, a plumed hat, and two big shawls of embroidered silk, one white and one black. In the store room of Odin Teatret I found a big velvet-bound book, a sword stick that concealed a long blade inside, and a bridal veil.

Slowly I incorporated these objects into the physical and vocal scores I had created, while at the same time leaving space for unexpected associations to emerge.

Then we went on tour again, and while still participating fully in all the activities of Odin Teatret, the figure of the woman with her bundle continued to mature within Jan and me.

After three years our work came to at a dead-end. We could not find a story that linked, like a string of pearls, the scenes of our montage. We sought help.

Every year I am responsible for the organisation of an Odin Week, sometimes even two weeks, where fifty participants get to know our work better by taking part in training and seeing all our work demonstrations and performances. There is also a daily meeting with Eugenio and another meeting, called the Odin Tradition, with one of the actors. During the Odin Weeks of 1998, 1999 and 2000, Jan and I chose this moment, the Odin Tradition, to present our montage on the theme of nostalgia as a work-in-progress. At the end of each presentation we asked spectators to tell us the story with which they had associated our work. We had many answers, but none were convincing enough.

Eugenio had seen our material many times over the years and had given us advice on how to proceed in the work.

In the Odin Week of February 2001, after the presentation of our montage one of the participants asked what kept Eugenio from turning this work into a performance. I replied that he did not have the time.

These words reached Eugenio's ears, and in the next Odin Week (which, uniquely, was held two weeks later) he wanted to see how our work had developed. Jan and I had more than an hour's worth of material consisting of dances, texts, music, lights, props, set and costumes. By now our montage had become like a plant that had grown so much that it had reached the ceiling: we had to take it outdoors or else it risked dying.

From my work diary:

> *Holstebro, 5 March 2001*
> *These were Eugenio's comments after seeing our montage:*
>   *The material is derived from work with props on an 'external' level.*
>   *You need to improvise with an internal process.*
>   *What I am seeing now is virtuosity, the material itself does not emerge.*
>   *What I am seeing is a film already structured in terms of actions and reactions.*
>   *All the scenes are too short, you need to do a scene that stays the same, but in which a small change occurs at the end that transforms everything.*
>   *You need to work on variations.*

You need to develop the rhythm of the entrance.
Is it possible to build a performance by doing an acoustic process only? Think of a dramaturgical soundtrack of Hamlet, create a theme, and then insert variations on the theme in the scene.
Work technically: find a theme starting from images. For example: what do I associate, on a sound level, with the sea?
Sound associations and visual associations.
Can I narrate a story on a visual level only?
What story could it be?
You are storytellers and every episode has a prologue.
Think of a variety show.
Every scene has to have a prelude, which can be rhythmic (but why is it rhythmic?).
Then associations have to emerge. Starting from the material, the first synopsis is reached.
The fact that there is now no connection between the episodes evokes the impression of madness, or of ceremony. In this case, for whom and against what is the ceremony?
Find how to use the suitcase without letting it remain just a suitcase.
When one is working blindly, one needs to have materials with different textures to avoid the monotony.

In that same month Eugenio gathered all the actors in his office to tell us the theme of the new group performance, the one which eventually became *Andersen's Dream* three years later.

In April, Eugenio informed Jan and me that he was ready to turn our montage into a performance. The story would be based on *Si sta facendo sempre più tardi*, a 'novel in the form of letters' by Antonio Tabucchi.[4] Jan and I had been hoping for quite some time that Eugenio would intervene in our work.

Our period of helplessness, when we could not find the story, was in any case an important experience for us.

Like the performances that Eugenio creates with the group, *Salt* had its origins in a theme – the one about nostalgia which Jan and I had explored together – and not just in a collage of material that emerged from the physical training, as had been the case with *Judith* whose theme was found by Eugenio only a month before the premiere.

In the eighteen months that passed between Eugenio's decision to direct *Salt* and its opening night, we continued to tour with *Mythos, Inside the Skeleton of the Whale, Ode to Progress,* and also to present our solo performances, work demonstrations and workshops, as well as our big projects likes Festuge, ISTA and Odin Week.

In the meantime we also had to create material for *Andersen's Dream*, which could involve travel and research periods away from home. It was for this reason that Torgeir and I travelled to Zanzibar in July 2002 to see the fifth Festival of the Dhow Countries that was taking place in Stone Town. I was returning to Africa after exactly twenty years, this time not to show my dances but to learn theirs. Once again, on the eve of the rehearsals of a new performance I felt the need to learn a new technique. I had daily two-hour classes with Zuhira and Jannette, two young dancers I had seen during the festival. I was particularly impressed by the great mobility of the pelvis and the agility of the legs during their dances. They jumped as if the earth was a trampoline and their steps had great elasticity. This was a completely unknown physical universe to me.

I have to consult my diaries of 2001 and 2002 to see how much time it took us to create *Salt*.

> 2001: August, two weeks; September, two weeks.
> 2002: March, three weeks; April–May, four weeks; June–July, three weeks; August–September, two weeks.

In a total of sixteen weeks of work, Eugenio transformed our montage into a performance with eight hundred kilogrammes of scenography. At the same time, the embryo of *Andersen's Dream* was growing in his mind and those of the actors.

The elaboration of *Salt*'s material was a particularly painful experience for me, perhaps because the creation process was already in an advanced state when the director intervened. Jan and I had grown fond of the solutions we had found. Texts, objects, musical instruments, elements of the set and songs that we loved were swept away by Eugenio. Result: insecurity. Now we had only questions and new tasks ahead of us.

For the first time in fifteen years I faced the challenge of a relatively long text. This was a need I had been nurturing for a long time.

Eugenio does not like to hear me speak in foreign languages in performances. He prefers that I express myself in my mother tongue, with the result that spectators frequently do not understand what I am saying. For this reason I often sing my texts, so that the emotive message of the words can be found in the colour of the song.

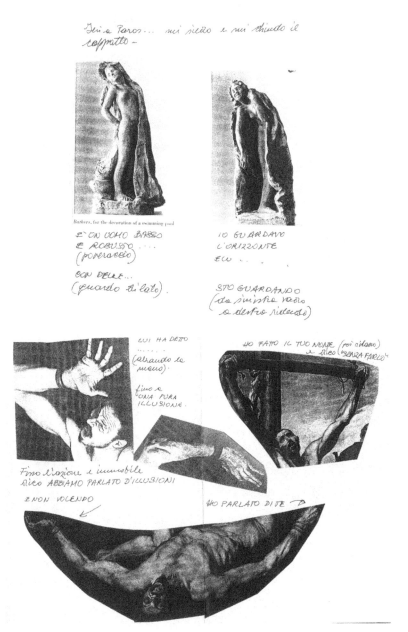

Pages from my work diary of *Salt*: juxtaposition of a text with a sequence of actions based on Rodin's statues and on crucifixion images.

140 The story and the training

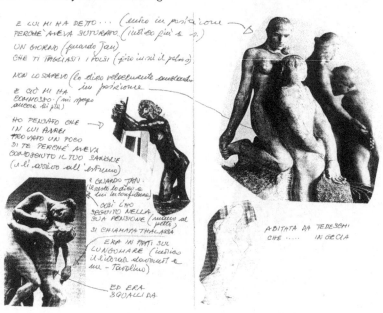

E LUI MI HA DETTO... (entro in posizione
PERCHE' AVEVA SUTURATO. (indico più o m.)
UN GIORNO (guardo Jan)
CHE TI TAGLIASTI I POLSI (giro in su il polso)

NON LO SAPEVO (lo dico velocemente guardando
                in posizione
E CIO' MI HA
COMMOSSO. (mi stringo
ancora di più)

HO PENSATO CHE
IN LUI AVREI
TROVATO UN POCO
DI TE PERCHE' AVEVA
CONOSCIUTO IL TUO SANGUE
(mi li arrivo all'estremo)

E GUARDO TAN.
(Ripeto lo dico a
lui in confidenza)

COSÌ L'HO
SEGUITO NELLA
SUA PENSIONE (mano al petto)
SI CHIAMAVA THALASSA

ERA IN FRTI SUL
LUNGOMARE (indico
il litorale davanti a
me - Tavolino)

ED ERA
SQUALLIDA

ABITATA DA TEDESCHI
CHE ...... IN GRECIA

LUI ERA GENTILE (mano
si. in posizione 5
(S)I È SPOGLIATO CON PUDORE
(mi giro e mano s. alle
mele.)
(E AVEVA UN MEMBRO....
(piano apro la mano s.
e guardo attraverso le
dita).
COME .... ATENE

NON VOLEVA TANTO
UNA DONNA, (scopro
il ginocchio)
HA SOPRATTUTTO PAROLE
PAROLE DI CONFORTO
(mentre accarezzo
la gamba).
- copro il ginocchio
con la mano sin -
PERCHE' ERA INFELICE
(vado coll'indice d.
alle bocce).

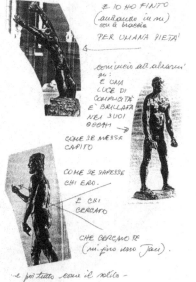

E IO HO FINTO
(andando in su
con le braccia
PER UMANA PIETA'

cominciai ad alzarmi
su:
E UNA
LUCE DI
COMPLICITÀ
È BRILLATA
NEI SUOI
OCCHI

COME SE AVESSE
CAPITO

COME SE SAPESSE
CHI ERO.

E CHI
CERCAVO

CHE CERCAVO TE
(mi giro verso Jan).

... e poi tutto come il solito -

During the rehearsals of *Salt* I experimented with various ways of saying the same text:

- following Jan's music but without singing the text (that is, finding the melody in the tonal qualities of the voice);
- creating a fixed sequence of vocal actions;
- ignoring Jan's music and saying the text as fast as I could while still being perfectly understandable;
- performing a series of actions based on some Rodin statues to underline the meaning of the text;
- assimilating all the physical actions, making them smaller, and letting Jan follow the dynamic of my text with his music.

We tried to find strategies for every part of the text to avoid what Eugenio called my 'butter voice'. I did not understand exactly what he meant by this, but it was clear that I had to find other vocal dynamics. Here are some examples of the strategies we tried out.

One day Eugenio gave me a theme for a vocal improvisation which he then told me to memorise. The following day he made me repeat a text in English by Jeanette Winterson (which I had used in my montage with Jan), asking me to use the melody from the previous day's vocal improvisation. This was a long process that took hours of work.

Then I had to apply the result of this work to an excerpt from Tabucchi, in Italian. We spent an entire afternoon recording the inflections of every word in the text of the scene we call 'Samarcanda'. An exhausting work. Then I had to memorise it: to learn it so well that I could 'forget' it afterwards.

The essential is what would remain.

On another occasion Eugenio asked me to do a vocal improvisation on the theme 'The Cat Purrs in the Street' and to memorise it. Then he told me to apply the result, saying a text and justifying the sounds of the original improvisation in the new context. In this way I could choose the associations I wanted to awaken in spectators through the inflections of my voice.

In between work periods on *Salt*, while on tour with other performances, I spent hours seeking new ways of saying the text.

Every time we started rehearsing again, Eugenio would cut a phrase here and a word there. Every day. It was difficult to remember which word to leave out: after repeating it for so long it had become part of an internal melody. It was like skipping a phrase in a story.

'Do not flatten the voice! Do vocal actions!', Eugenio would say.

That was exactly what I thought I was doing, but the result of 'translating' physical action into vocal action (for example, throwing a stone) was not the desired one: I was repeating my clichés.

May 2002, another pause in the construction of *Salt*: touring with other performances. We resumed the work at the end of June. Eugenio changed our set design: he wanted a circle of stars hanging in the centre of the space and so had a copper circle made with a three-metre diameter and inset halogen spotlights.

Jan and I had originally used only candles to light our montage. 'How do you justify the presence of candles in a performance?' Eugenio asked. Only one candle made it in the end, the one which Jan lights at the beginning and which shines throughout the performance on a small table next to where he sits.

For a while we kept the footlights: a row of water-filled glasses with lights floating in them. Eugenio wanted the lights to go off at the end without our direct intervention. To extinguish the flames we devised a bar with holes which, when turning, let fall a shower of salt. The glasses with the lights were removed some days later, but the curtain of salt still closes the performance.

Eugenio wanted Jan's costume to be a white suit with a Panama hat. His face had to be covered by a cloth, like one does with the dead, and when Jan took it away at the end of the performance Eugenio wanted to see his face covered with worms. We even tried to put the worms under the cloth. Luckily the worms did not live long in the jar where we kept them, and Jan was spared this distress.

After some months Eugenio removed the cloth from Jan's face, but had him play with his back to the public. Then he turned him round once again to face the spectators but placed him beyond the dance carpet that delineated my space, asking him to always keep his head lowered in a way that covered the face with the wide brim of the hat.

Eugenio said: 'Jan's music is the voice of his character. This is the story of a woman who searches for her lover. Did he flee? Is he dead? Did he kill himself? This is the story of a ghost who loves a woman.'

Eugenio tried hard to insert a letter in the performance. He had me pull one out from a pocket in my coat and read it like the opening lines of the performance. He had me find one in a book. He had me take from the suitcase a number of letters bound together with a red ribbon. In the final version there is only the one which Jan finds at the end of the performance in the stretch of salt that separates us from the audience. A letter full of the salt of my tears.

I created new material from improvisations based on the themes provided by Eugenio. Once again, to avoid my personal clichés, I memorised images of paintings and statues as a starting point for creating sequences of actions. I learned them, and Eugenio broke them up in little fragments and had phrases pasted on them.

I needed time to memorise the new version of the text with its new physical and vocal actions. However, the unrelenting daily cuts kept it foreign to me: I had to 'think it' all the time, and to think the actions. The montage never had enough time to become 'organic' because I did not manage to digest it before it was changed yet again. Frustration reigned. Raúl Iaiza was the assistant director of the performance.[5] His patience and musical expertise were indispensible for *Salt*.

The performance went through several metamorphoses and took us to places we had not imagined at the beginning. Even the set design changed.

During rehearsals, the big copper circle with inset halogen lights that had been conceived, built and inserted in the scenic space was removed. A harp with strings that 'broke' on their own, conceived of and built at great cost, was used for a while and then discarded – just as all the hours of improvisations were forgotten when, to give the text more prominence in certain instances, a state of near-immobility was chosen. Of the seven suitcases I had originally used and which constituted my scenography from which emerged all the objects that I used in the original montage, only one remained: the smallest. Half the instruments that Jan had learned to play after hours and hours of practice never made it to the final version of *Salt*.

A waste? The poet writes a thousand pages to publish a book with a hundred. A waste?

Perhaps waste is our method.

Notes

1 *Salt*, 2002–present. Actors: Roberta Carreri and Jan Ferslev. Text by Antonio Tabucchi. Scenic adaptation and direction: Eugenio Barba.
2 *The Whispering Winds in Theatre and Dance*, 1996–present. Actors: Roberta Carreri, Iben Nagel Rasmussen, Julia Varley and Torgeir Wethal (until 2010). In 2011, Tage Larsen and Augusto Omolù joined as actors, the latter until 2013. Musicians: Kai Bredholt, Jan Ferslev and Frans Winther.
3 Jan Ferslev is a Danish musician and actor who joined Odin Teatret in 1987. In addition to *Salt* and *Itsi Bitsi*, he has taken part in all group performances since 1987.
4 Antonio Tabucchi, *It is Getting Later All the Time*, trans. Alastair McEwan (New York: New Directions, 2006). The text of the performance is based on the chapter 'Letter to Write', pp. 209–14.

5 Raúl Iaiza is an Argentinian flautist and director. In 1994 he founded the theatre group La Madrugada in Milan. Apart from *Salt*, he was assistant director to Eugenio Barba in three other performances by Odin Teatret: *Andersen's Dream* (2004–11), *Don Giovanni all'Inferno* (2006–present), and *The Chronic Life* (2011–present). In *Don Giovanni all'Inferno* he was also responsible for the selection and musical arrangement of Mozart's music.

26 Our chronic life[1]

We have just eaten supper and are still at table when I mention to Torgeir my dream of having a family grave for Odin Teatret here in Holstebro, where we've worked and lived for a lifetime. It is 2003 and we are working on the performance *Andersen's Dream*. For the creation of my physical scores I have bought an urn, my own urn, and I have created a scene with ashes. Seated on the other side of the table, Torgeir listens to me and smiles in silence. Death is simply a lack of life; for him only life exists.

The beginning of a new performance has often been compared to the beginning of a new life. Our performances have only ever been conceived with just the actors and the director present, no one else, in an atmosphere full of trepidation and intimacy. For *Andersen's Dream*, Eugenio had seeded our fantasy in diverse places: in his office in Holstebro, in a hotel room in Moscow, on a restaurant terrace in Cagliari.

Eugenio's 'verbal improvisations' have the gift of being so precise and yet so vast as to be able to stimulate the imagination and awaken the interest of every actor. We are all so very different from each other, with long experience behind us and a sense of weariness weighing heavily on our shoulders. We carry on because we cannot help it. Is it vocation? Sometimes the waters are disturbed as if by the violent thrashing of a fish trying to liberate itself from the hook. Fits of anger. Against our own destiny?

9 April 2011, and *Andersen's Dream* ends with a surprise in Bogotá with Eugenio's declaration at the end of the performance, directly addressing the spectators: 'You have witnessed the very last performance of *Andersen's Dream*'. For the first time in the history of Odin Teatret Eugenio closes a production on the stage, in front of the spectators. The axe has fallen. A big tree has been cut down in order

to give more light to a younger one which, two weeks earlier, appeared to have taken root.

It is 2008. Eugenio sets aside the whole of February to begin work on a new performance whose provisional title is *XL*, Extra Large. He decides to start rehearsals in the theatre's smallest working room. We, on the other hand, are many in number. Entering the blue room, from the left and seated along all four walls, are Roberta, Jan, Iben, Tage, Julia, Frans, Kai, Eugenio, Torgeir, Sofia, the literary advisor Nando Taviani, the actor-technician Donald Kitt, the technician Fausto Pro, and the three assistants to the director, Raul Iaiza, Pierangelo Pompa and Ana Woolf. Also present are Tina Nielsen (one of Odin Teatret's former actors who has become a Protestant minister), Anna Stigsgaard (assistant director for *Andersen's Dream*), and the young English director Max Webster.

For the first time Eugenio describes to us the theme of a new performance in the presence of other people. Every moment of the creation of this performance will be witnessed by others. Is it to help Eugenio? Or is it to help us, the actors?

5 February 2008. The blue room is the only working room with windows. Outside, sprinkled with snow, the thin, black branches of the birch trees stand out. I am expecting a new beginning, but when Eugenio opens his mouth he confronts us once again with a funeral. This time, however, it is not that of a song or an idea – it is his own.

Eugenio says: 'One day you come to the theatre and someone tells you that I've died. In a letter I ask you to organise my funeral with what you know I love. You will be able to converse with me, tell me things you have never told me. For so many years you've all struggled against being crushed by the Angel. You must create a scene in which you show the struggle between Jacob and the Angel. Tell a story full of horror and humour, a story about me, in which you must only refer to me as "him", never "you". You must each prepare your own ceremony, in just a few minutes. You decide how. You will have to direct your colleagues. Sofia, on the other hand, has another story. She has come to look for her father.' This event is the pivotal point around which all of our stories will intertwine. Our pole star is the theme of integration. As usual, the theme for Eugenio's performance is something topical, burning.

How can we avoid repeating ourselves, after so many years of working with the same people? How do we avoid reverting to our own clichés? Every time we have started working on a new performance we have tried to find different strategies to answer these questions. Now, however, instead of trying to escape from the past, we are to dig up fragments of performances that are extinct: scenes, costumes, objects, songs. Like an organic theatre, we recycle our past, grinding it up to extract a new performance. Everything we pick out is placed in the 'store-room' at the centre of the back wall in the blue room.

We start out from what we already have, offering each item as a gift, a journey into the land of memory.

At the same time we hear Eugenio saying to us: 'When you improvise, you are repeating your mannerisms. We have to be able to rid ourselves of these. Details are essential and it is on these that we will work. You do not have to prepare new scores, but you do have to plan strategies to escape from your clichés.' Lolito (the angel from the performance *The Land of Nod*) and the scene with the coins from *Min Fars Hus* are among the first fragments to appear. Lolito dominates in the 'store-room' where the objects, masks, puppets and musical instruments are stacked. A large quantity of coins fills the space. They are presented as small offerings or a reward for our own actions, but also for those of the other actors. When dropped into metal bowls they produce sounds and rhythms.

'The performance is a great river kept alive by its tributaries: dance and music. But the way we bring the coins to life and cause them to resound is yet another tributary. This performance must be a dance marathon and nobody on the stage should sit still and do nothing,' Eugenio says.

12 February 2008. In the centre of the space we are greeted by a large rectangular object covered by a cloth. Eugenio says: 'Under this cloth there are two ideas; one is mine and the other is Luca Ruzza's'. The cloth is removed and underneath there is a transparent coffin, like the one in *Snow White*. It is full of water, and in it swims an eel. Eugenio asks Sofia to climb into the coffin. Her body sinks gently into the water. Her hair floats and billows while the eel slides along her legs. It seems to be in its element. When Eugenio asks Sofia to come out of the water she re-emerges, shivering from the cold and a sense of repulsion.

The space that Eugenio wants to use measures five metres by three metres. Tiny. Even our smallest action becomes deafening. We are used to big spaces, and the old circus horse within each of us makes me and my colleagues exaggerate. Only Torgeir works in harmony with the space: controlled, always reflective, totally present. Not a single detail escapes him. This is in contrast to many of us, who are so intent on finding the answers to Eugenio's requests that we often close our ears and minds to what the others are doing. Torgeir appears always to listen.

Every day, and always in the same order of presentation, we repeat each of the actors' proposed scores, together with Nando's. Every day Eugenio makes changes, proposing something new.

During his scene, Tage asks us to repeat phrases that we have heard Eugenio repeat ad nauseam over the years. What springs to my mind is, 'This performance has to fit in a suitcase.'

After three weeks of seclusion, the performance lasts eighty minutes. In our 'store-room', fragments of old performances are stacked together with new ideas. We put them back into the 'crystal coffin'. We interrupt the rehearsals to go on tour with our repertoire. We do not know when we will be working on *XL* again. Maybe in a year. In the meantime, we must create our own characters and at least half an hour of 'musical texture'. I do not have any ideas. I just need to escape from myself.

Coming out of the cocoon of the blue room doesn't mean coming out of the creative state in which we have been immersed. The performance keeps on growing inside me, provoking sudden desires. In April we're on tour in Istanbul. Torgeir and I wander around discovering this extraordinary city suspended between two cultures. Our path takes us to a road full of music shops and I am drawn to one which sells *bindir*, big tambourines made with a seasoned wood frame and goatskin. Some of them are really beautiful. I go in and start trying them out for sound. Some are less striking in appearance but have a wonderful sound, whereas others that are more beautiful produce a sound that is rather flat. Torgeir is happy to wait for me, reading a newspaper while drinking a beer at a café opposite. After two hours I come out of the shop beaming with a splendid *bindir* in my arms, without even asking myself why.

In June Torgeir and I are in Athens, partly for work and partly on holiday. Walking through Plaka, Torgeir stops suddenly in front of a little shop full of souvenirs where he sees a small instrument hanging. There are others, but it is the one which first caught Torgeir's attention that we end up buying. It is the simplest-looking one, but it has the broadest range of tone and the clearest sound. Torgeir says, 'You should use this in the new performance.' The *baglama*, which is what it is called, is so small that it can fit in my hand luggage. From that moment on, it accompanied me around the world.

During a tour in Peru in the autumn of 2008 I buy some indigenous masks made of thin metal mesh: two female and two male. The female one, with green eyes and pink cheeks, looks completely different from me, and that is why it is my favourite. At the market in Ayacucho I buy two aprons, like the ones worn by the Indian women there, one with red and white stripes and the other with green and white stripes. They have big pockets in which there is room for lots of ideas. In December Torgeir and I go on tour to Kuala Lumpur. Torgeir seems slower than usual. On the last day of the tour we sit next to each other having a Chinese foot massage. At the end of the session the masseur, with a very serious face, says to Torgeir in halting English, 'Your body is very tired.' His statement doesn't surprise us, but the tone of his voice worries us. From that moment Torgeir starts to stop smoking, cutting down by one cigarette a day. By Easter he has completely stopped, and he says to me, 'How strange, I don't miss smoking at all.'

January 2009. A winter of snow and blue skies. I choose to withdraw to create my individual scores in Sanjukta's tower, surrounded by windows, light and solitude. I climb upstairs with a red suitcase full of objects and instruments, CDs and books of poetry. Timidly I begin to fill the silence, playing my *bindir*. I explore its different possibilities by holding it in different ways, and at a certain point the tambourine becomes a tray.

To play the *baglama* I put on white gloves, whose fingers I have cut off. The *baglama* is a secret that I share only with Torgeir. I do not want anybody to know that I'm learning to play it, but after two weeks I need some help and Jan gives me some precious advice.

At home I find some old keys in a drawer. I hang them around my neck with a ribbon. In my dressing room I find an old hand-mirror that was given to me as a present long ago. I use it to put on my Peruvian mask and a platinum blond wig with a page-boy cut that I bought years ago in Hong Kong. I look into the mirror and I don't recognise myself: it is me, and yet it isn't me. It is fantastic to feel free from the slavery of my own appearance. I think of Uma Thurman in *Pulp Fiction*. It is strange because in that film her hair was black. Quentin Tarantino. Associations. I listen to myself and let myself be guided by associations, however banal they might seem. Our work resides in the elaboration of associations. *Pulp Fiction* takes me to an American diner. Waitresses, stories that are both banal and tragic. The tragedy of everyday life, or the everyday nature of tragedy? How many women with tragic destinies serve us coffee with a smile? I put on a 1950s dress, green with white spots, and on top of it the Peruvian apron with red and white stripes. I find a pair of red patent leather shoes with a white bow and black-and-white striped heels in a magazine and I order them through the internet. The result is a costume which is decidedly optimistic.

In Sanjukta's tower I go on a quest for thoughts, ideas. I do this by examining the objects that I brought with me. I give myself a new challenge: to create melodies with my *baglama* – melodies for texts written in Danish. I choose some of Janina Kats's poetry and I set it to music. Eugenio hates hearing me speak Danish. Why do I do it? Because it is what I need to do at this moment, in order not to recognise myself. And if I were to go in the opposite direction? I remember the songs of my youth. I sing Lucio Battisti and Milly, accompanying myself on the *bindir*. I know these songs are far too well-known and worn-out, but they are what have sprung to mind here and now, and I am in this here and now. I need to let my thoughts blossom. My task is to discover new possibilities and, if I can, to surprise the director. Then Eugenio will decide what will work best for the performance.

Torgeir works in another part of the theatre. At home we never talk about our individual work. We like the idea of surprising each other.

4 May 2009. We resume work on *XL*. We are told that the title of the new performance is going to be *The Chronic Life*. 'Another of Eugenio's oxymorons,' I think to myself when I hear it for the first time. It does not strike any chords with me. Maybe it is simply inspired by his mother's fate, a lady in her nineties, bed-ridden, with no memory, and who does not even have the pleasure of recognising her own son.

We have had more than a year to create our characters – the characters in a performance for which we do not know the story, the context or the text. Helped by Pierangelo's video recording, we repeat the last scene and then the entire montage. On day two in the blue room, we are greeted by the new stage set: a floor made of wooden boards with lights that shine through the gaps between them. With a bottle of Polish vodka, Eugenio christens the set 'Medusa's raft' and says that in this performance he does not want visible spotlights. He only wants candles, light sticks and ecological torches. We do not have to worry too much about the technological side of things. No Jesper Kongshaug light designs. The lighting has to be imaginative and poor. Eugenio informs us that dance, like the music, is one of the central themes of the performance, constantly re-emerging as a form of thoroughbass. Another central element will be the fact of being lame. We have to practise hobbling around. This small physical limitation will help us overcome our clichés and will give us new rhythmic possibilities, Eugenio says.

Every day we take turns to demonstrate the results of our research into our characters, our materials, the 'sound textures'. When it is my turn I present two characters: Sugar and Lola. They both wear a Peruvian metal mesh mask and a wig: one is blonde and the other is brunette. Sugar plays the *baglama*, Lola the *bindir*. For months now, both in hotel rooms and at home, I have been practising to learn to play the musical pieces on the *baglama* without looking at the chords. Eugenio chooses Sugar and asks me to write her biography. Easy. Her real name: Norma Jones, American, born in Utah, the daughter of an Italian woman and a Danish man. Age sixty. From seven to thirteen years of age she suffers sexual abuse at the hands of her stepfather. By sixteen she is pregnant by one of her classmates. She leaves school. She escapes and goes to live with her grandmother in Louisiana where her son is born. She becomes a waitress in a diner. She gets married and has a daughter. When her daughter is seven, Norma realises that her husband is sexually abusing the girl. (At first I think she should kill her husband, but then I remember that in the US there is the death penalty for this type of crime). In the meantime, during a car chase, the police kill her fifteen-year-old son, who was escaping on a stolen motorbike. Sugar's passion is singing. Eugenio listens and then suggests that Sugar might have cancer of the throat, and it is this that distorts her voice.

When Torgeir shows us his character, I discover that he too is 'American' and wears red shoes. Might this be because of the films we watch together? Or maybe it is the result of our desire to move as far as we can from the image we have of ourselves, from what we identify ourselves with? Torgeir's character is an Eastern European spy in the United States. He wears a blue suit with red Converse canvas shoes, a red T-shirt and a red baseball cap. Torgeir's material is not very dynamic in the space, but it has a great interior dynamism. His character attempts suicide in many different ways. He makes repeated attempts but always, at the last minute, life is stronger than his desire to die. Is this the chronic life? Torgeir is a very refined actor. Acting has always been his greatest passion. Over the years some of us have wondered what we might have done instead of working at Odin Teatret. I have never heard Torgeir asking himself this question. He has always embraced his destiny. King of the present, his eyes and heart always wide open to the world, with light steps he has left deep footprints in the hearts of his spectators.

We start working every morning at eight o'clock in the black room with two hours of 'plant nursery'. Here we have the possibility of making the characters we have created grow. In the 'plant nursery' I visit the space of the various objects:

THE TRAY/*bindir* – which I use as a waitress and to accompany myself when singing. While carrying it I develop Sugar's different styles of walking.

THE KEYS. I ask Torgeir's sister, who at present lives in Yemen, to send me some old keys. They arrive: big and rough, strong and heavy. The idea of the keys is linked to the theme of the door in *Kaosmos*. It occurs to me that Torgeir's character in *Kaosmos* was the man who does not want to die, while in this performance he is the man who does want to die.

THE HANDKERCHIEFS. From the pocket of my apron, a handkerchief protrudes. I use it for polishing, to crush things, to dry tears and to say goodbye… The handkerchiefs increase in number and I use them to tie my wrists and ankles, to gag and to blindfold myself. I start cleaning glasses and windows.

THE MIRROR. The hand-mirror that I used when adjusting my mask and wig, I now use to illuminate or attract my fellow actors.

To give body to the dance marathon, we take turns in the 'plant nursery' to learn the steps of the tango and the milonga in the arms of Ana Woolf.

My character is starting to come out of her 'bubble' and to interact with the other characters. I use the keys to open up their chests and extract their hearts, like a good heartbreaker. I use the hand-mirror to confront them with their own images and defects.

Eugenio suggests that as a waitress I should introduce food that I can offer to the other characters. Food that produces a sound and can be woven into the fabric of sounds being created, together with those of the coins and the dance steps, and the objects of the other characters: Julia's playing cards, Iben's sword, Kai and Sofia's bucket and broom, Tage's book, Jan's belt and Torgeir's broken guitar.

Erect and determined, Sugar walks with small quick steps. Her improvisations have a certain dreaminess about them, where the suggestion of past violence and abuse is ever present. But in her reality there is only space for work and singing.

13 May. The performance space is transformed drastically. Butcher's hooks have now appeared in the 'storeroom'. Objectively they are harmless, immobile, hanging high up and attached to a rope made of tow, yet they are decidedly disturbing in their starkness. Objects,

instruments, and puppets are to hang from these hooks. Suddenly our raft feels threatening.

At the end of this period of rehearsals, I have the feeling that my character is not really necessary to this performance. I have created it to break free from my own mannerisms and to help Eugenio escape from his, but the truth is that Eugenio does not seem to be interested in breaking out of his clichés. On the contrary, he seems to be reaffirming and strengthening them. That is why my character, which is so 'different', does not seem to work, in the sense that it does not have a function in Eugenio's dramaturgy. But in his talk at the end of the second period of rehearsals for *The Chronic Life*, Eugenio surprises me when he draws this conclusion, saying, 'Now we have the space, the characters. The story is clear: how does a person become integrated? We have Julia's character who allows herself to be integrated, and Sofia's who refuses to be integrated. We are free. However, we feel that there is no escape route because we cannot find the key to open the door. The clinking coins are part of the musical symphony that accompanies the performance, and food is the other element. In this society we eat when we're not hungry and we drink when we're not thirsty.' So there I am: Sugar's keys and food are essential after all.

Eugenio leaves us with individual tasks to fulfil before the next phase of rehearsals in October.

The third phase starts on 5 October 2009. We have moved to the white room to allow space for the building of the audience's tribune. Elena Flores, with her talent and experience as a violinist, has also become part of the ensemble of the *The Chronic Life*, replacing Frans Winther who is no longer in the performance.

Eugenio sums up the themes of the performance and asks Julia to change her costume. Her character should no longer be a man, but a woman instead. We all find ourselves in a moment of openness and almost no one protests.

In the morning we continue with the 'plant nursery' and then with the rehearsals, which are always run-throughs, interrupted by Eugenio's corrections. Sometimes there are periods of tension because we all want to do our best and to use every instant to work on the music or the texts. But in this creative process we need to be aware of the moments when Eugenio is looking for solutions, taking risks. This is when we all need to pay attention, even if the particular scene does not involve us personally. Eugenio needs our help in the form of collective concentration. Torgeir is an expert at this. During run-throughs and work on single scenes he never thinks of his own work, but remains focused on what Eugenio is doing with his colleagues.

Eugenio asks me to develop the theme of the door/key and to write texts on this theme.

Halfway through October Eugenio starts working on the spectators' tribune, making it an integral part of the set. Once again we have arrived at the point at which the 'boys' become excited about finding technical solutions, and we 'girls' become bored to death. We decide that the next phase will be in February 2010.

Two weeks after the end of the third phase of *The Chronic Life*, Torgeir and I discover that the reason for his lack of energy is probably due to a cancer. We listen to the word 'metastasis' spoken for the first time by the head of the respiratory department at Holstebro Hospital on 29 October 2009. It is the morning of Eugenio's seventy-third birthday. At noon, together with the other members of Odin Teatret, we sit at a lavishly set table listening to speeches, laughter and songs. Eugenio is resplendent at the head of the table. Kai sings a song by Leonard Cohen: *May everyone live, may everyone die, Hello my love, my love goodbye.* I blink away my tears while Torgeir and I hold hands tightly, hidden under the table. Who are we, we humans, who can conceive the idea of God and yet be so inhuman with our fellow men; we who can laugh while in pain and cry with joy?

In the morning of 10 November we go to the Town Hall to arrange a date for our wedding after we have lived together for long enough to be celebrating our silver anniversary. Then we go to the hospital to hear the results of the liver biopsy carried out the previous week: small cell lung cancer with secondary metastases in the liver and a vertebra. Now that we have the diagnosis we need to find the cure. At the end of the afternoon Torgeir asks me to summon all our colleagues to Odin Teatret's library for a glass of sparkling wine. Then, raising his glass, he announces his illness and the imminent beginning of his treatment.

19 November, 8.30 am: our wedding at the Holstebro Town Hall. 10.30 am: first session of chemotherapy in Herning.

It is 2010. Eugenio decides not to use the month of February for rehearsing *The Chronic Life* as planned, but instead to rework all of Odin Teatret's ensemble performances, without the presence of Torgeir. Eugenio wants Torgeir to focus totally on his treatment and not take part in the impending tours with the old performances.

Torgeir, with his usual ease and kindness, helps us in this harrowing process.

We postpone the next phase of *The Chronic Life* until May.

From the 10 to 26 May we work in the white room. Torgeir wakes up late and does not come to the theatre to work in the 'plant nursery' or for the first morning run-through. During the midday break I go home and pick him up. For the first time in its history, all the members of Odin Teatret have decided to have lunch together to spend more time with Torgeir. We take turns in pairs to cook. Torgeir takes part in the afternoon run-through. Eugenio creates new scenes and keeps making radical changes. He decides that Sugar should speak Romanian. My texts are translated. Eugenio asks me to sing a song while I lay flowers on the coffin. And Sugar sings: *I wanna die easy when I die.* Eugenio says that he cannot find a place in the performance for the theme of the key, so I abandon the material that I had prepared with the Yemeni keys. During morning rehearsals, for the sake of continuity, Eugenio asks me to play the part of Torgeir. This means that for me every rehearsal is different. But for the painstaking presence of Ana Woolf, who constantly tells me what to do, I would never have been able to remember all the changes suggested by Eugenio. Eugenio also gives some of Torgeir's tasks to the others.

The last run-through, which is to be filmed, happens in the afternoon and Torgeir takes part in it. In the confusion Kai says Torgeir's text by mistake – as he usually does in the morning rehearsal – before Torgeir, with the gun in his hand, has a chance to speak. After the rehearsal I knock at Torgeir's dressing room door. I find him seated at his desk. 'How do you feel?'

'It made me feel good, but I was slow.'

'Your character is slow.'

'Yes, but it was *me* that was slow.'

Then he gives me the gun and says, 'Give it to whoever has to use it after me.'

A month later, on 27 June, Torgeir peacefully stops breathing, after not even two days in hospital. The three women he loved the most in his adult life were at his side, all the time.

The fifth phase of *The Chronic Life* takes place in autumn 2010.

In September I prepare a scene with Jan. It was one of the tasks that Eugenio had set us. I choose to make Sugar sing *Stand by your Man*. We start with a series of embraces that develop into a struggle in which Jan plays his instrument and I use my dusting cloths and handkerchiefs.

When we start work again on 29 September we find that the set has been moved to the red room. We have once again ended up in the biggest room of our theatre.

Instead of crunchy food, Eugenio asks me to use bread. Instead of offering it to my colleagues, I now have to eat it myself. In addition to the two suicide attempts that I have already inherited directly from Torgeir's character, Eugenio asks me to add a third. I propose eating a glass, but this is not possible while I am wearing a mask. As a result, Eugenio decides to sacrifice the mask with which my character had started out. But I do not want to go back to being myself! So I decide to use green contact lenses and wear heavy make-up. Once again the miracle happens: I look at myself in the mirror and I do not recognise myself. Now I am ready to give up my mask. I sing a new song while I use the azure wings: *What a Wonderful World*. I sing it blindfolded before the second suicide attempt. Thus, Sugar has not only inherited Torgeir's absurd habit but also his implacable optimism.

I carry on finding different moments and ways to eat bread. In the end I just feel sick. That's it! Sugar is bulimic; therefore she eats all the time and then vomits. Perfectly in keeping with her story.

At the end of this phase we are due to present the rehearsals as a 'work in progress' at the Grotowski Institute in Wrocław. For this reason, from the 20 October we interrupt the 'plant nursery' to concentrate on individual scenes. Eugenio continues to experiment with the space, placing actors on the stairs and among the audience. The problem is that we cannot take up the spectators' seats.

In Wrocław, Eugenio works on the performance in the presence of forty students. One day he completely changes the space, opening it up for the entire length of the room. We find ourselves moving in the familiar river between two banks of spectators.

The fifth phase ends like this: opening up the space once again.

The sixth phase of *The Chronic Life* takes place in 2011 within the time frame of February and March. At this point Eugenio calls (once again) on Jesper Kongshaug to correct the light design for the performance. The performance needs his intervention to soar to another level. Jesper is both a genius and very straightforward at the same time. Just what we need.

The end of the performance changes a few times. Now we see a ray of hope, thanks to the simple and fresh presences of Sofia and Elena.

Eugenio's patience sometimes seems to me to be superhuman. He can wait years for results that he has no guarantee of achieving. He does it because he cannot help himself. There is absolutely no doubt about Eugenio's intelligence, but there is also *another* kind of intelligence that guides him.

Eugenio chains Jan to his electric guitar. His character is now a rock musician, and so he cannot play the 'folk' instruments that he had proposed during the development of the performance. In one scene Eugenio asks Jan to fall onto his back with the electric guitar on top of him. Not once, not twice, not even three times, but repeatedly. I shudder. Jan is in his sixties and does not have any training as a clown or a stuntman. He is a musician. In an effort to protect his instrument, he ends up tearing a muscle and the pain stays with him throughout the rehearsal period, considerably limiting his possibilities. But he carries on. Like me, like the others. Because we can't help it. Others have left, but we have stayed, embracing our destiny.

3 July 2011. A year ago we were celebrating Torgeir's funeral. The birth of *The Chronic Life* runs parallel to his illness and his death. In this performance, for me his absence is intensely present. My character has inherited an essential part of his character.

The self-destructiveness of some of Torgeir's characters was the fruit of an exuberance for life. It appears grotesque and cruel that an actor, at the end of his life, should create a character with a suicidal mania. Like a successful cross between the Buddha and Prince Myskin, Torgeir persisted in a serene optimism which filled him with light until his very last breath. I, who shared the last twenty-eight years of his life, never heard him utter a single word about his own death.

Torgeir started Odin Teatret with Eugenio in 1964, and in May 2010 he inaugurated the Odin Teatret family grave. There is space for twelve people, but if needs be, we will squeeze up and make room for others, just like at birthday parties.

Note

1   This chapter has been translated from Italian by Elena Masoero and Kemal Ibrahim, and edited by Frank Camilleri.

27 Metamorphosis

I never imagined that the creation of *Traces in the Snow* in 1998 would have led to the interruption of my training for such a long period. Today I can see that it was the logical consequence for having 'dramatised' the training in *Judith* and in the work demonstration. This pause was very useful for me. The time that I previously reserved for training was now dedicated to the organisation of my solo tours, something that was completely new to me. I learned how to typewrite, do budgets and formulate proposals.

When I agreed to write this book, I did not know that Guendalina Ravazzoni's photos of *Traces in the Snow* would be the documentation of the last time I was able to execute the physical exercises in slow motion.

I began experiencing serious back problems in January 2006 during our Copenhagen tour of *Andersen's Dream*. An MRI scan revealed the cause: a dorsal disc hernia between the fifth and sixth cervical vertebrae. Quite a rare occurrence. Geronimo's fall from the tightrope in Aarhus in 1979 had made itself felt once again. Crisis. How could I keep doing *Judith*, *Traces in the Snow* and all the other performances?

During the Odin Week of September 2006 I had to revise all the scores in my performances and adapt them to my new physical condition. I was afraid that the changes I was forced to make would compromise the scores' impact. My morale was very low. Today I feel comfortable and confident in all my roles. The old Noh theatre masters taught that, on stage, you have to be ninety percent present in what you are doing and ten percent aware of what is happening around you. To this I had to add another ten percent of my awareness not to hurt myself.

The significance of training changes over the years, because the needs of the group and of the individual actor change with the passing of time.

In my first years at Odin Teatret, training was a daily confrontation with tasks I did not know how to execute. Learning how to do the acrobatic exercises helped me to face my limits and my desire to go beyond them. The road of my apprenticeship was paved with physical pain and tears of powerlessness.

With hindsight, I can see how this process contained one of the essential aspects of training: apart from discovering new and unexpected energies in myself and developing a more informed physical intelligence, through daily repetition I also asserted my need to be exactly where I was.

Later on, training became my secret garden, the space where I could give vent to my creative need, fulfilling ideas and aspirations that did not find a place in Eugenio's ensemble performances. All the material that led to my solo performances was born in my secret garden.

Even today, despite spending more time sitting in front of a computer in my dressing-room, training continues to have the same connotation of 'personal luxury' for me, a time of research dedicated to my own growth.

In our group there have been excellent actors, like Torgeir Wethal, who did not train after the first ten years in the group.

Being good in training does not necessarily mean being a good actor, just like being a good actor does not necessarily mean being a good teacher.

Training is a base for the actor, just like knowing how to use a hammer and a chisel is a base for a sculptor. The actor then needs to use these acquired skills to render his or her presence believable on stage; just like the sculptor uses the ability to handle hammer and chisel to create statutes that are eternally alive. But not all sculptors who know how to use hammer and chisel reach this objective, just like not all actors who are good in training are believable on stage.

Training has also helped to keep our group together in periods when there were no performances to present, such as in 1966 when Odin Teatret moved from Norway to Denmark, or in 1974 when it relocated for five months to Italy in Carpignano Salentino. In April 1979, two days before leaving for Germany with *Brecht's Ashes* which we had only just finished, Else Marie abandoned the performance. After Eugenio made his bewildered announcement and dismissed us for the rest of the day, we went to the workspace to train. Doing concrete actions helped us cope with the shock.

Undoubtedly, training is essential for a certain kind of theatre. However, it was during rehearsals that Eugenio effectively formed his actors with a patience that I still consider extraordinary, even if gesticulation and raising his voice are not alien to his temperament as a director.

The objective of training is to help the actor be believable on stage by doing an action in a manner that is true and not mechanical; that is, to avoid mere *repetition* and to inhabit the action, modulating, phrasing and enjoying it. If the actor does not manage to enjoy what she is doing, the spectator will not enjoy seeing it.

Training is a long journey that leads to the overcoming of the mind/body, thought/action dichotomy, making one feel sufficiently in control of the situation to play with the spectators' attention, stimulating their senses and imagination.

When I began training I *thought my body*. To move my elbow I had to think the action first and then my mind provided the elbow with the impulse to move. I even had to look at my elbow to see how it reacted to my thought. With the passing of time I acquired the capacity to *think with my body* – that is to say, to translate my intentions immediately into actions.

Once this identity of body and mind was obtained, I subsequently arrived at *physically thinking the body*, that is, to visualise its image in action in the space. This has made it possible for me, even in a hotel room, to create my scenic proposals by starting from small impulses.

Over the years, the training has followed my professional development and passed through various metamorphoses. There have been moments of crisis, growth and change. But training has been a *tao* for me, a *modus vivendi*, a way of putting myself at stake and being in dialogue with my profession, so that I do not get swallowed up by routine, so that I do not lose my sense of *wonder*.

'How many sacrifices!' I have often heard exclaimed by people who studied our history. 'Sacrifice' does not exist in my vocabulary. Nobody forced me to be an actress with Odin Teatret.

The day after I saw *Min Fars Hus* for the first time, some spectators present for the public morning training session asked about the method of Odin Teatret. Eugenio evaded the trap of stating his method, avoiding their need to label him.

I saw the training of Iben and Jens and I was not bored; I saw the performance and I was not bored. My senses were stimulated, my imagination was engaged. Eugenio managed to create believable actors. Believable also beyond the performance. Their way of living and relating to the work was for me the exemplification of a coherent and full life.

If we have a method, I think it is contained in the phrases Eugenio says at the end of the film on Odin Teatret's physical training: 'Whatever you do, do it with all of your whole self. It sounds like, and is, a facile and rhetorical phrase. Anybody can say it. But we have only one possibility: to live it, to carry it out in our daily acts. And training reminds us of this.'[1]

At this moment, my training is to capture and translate into written words the core of a professional life that I have chosen in order to escape the ambiguity of words.

This is part of that tradition of transmitting one's experience, to which I feel I belong.

Note

1 *Physical Training at Odin Teatret*, directed by Torgeir Wethal (Odin Teatret Film, 1972), produced in collaboration with the Italian public broadcasting corporation RAI. The transcript of Eugenio Barba's commentary in the film can be found in Eugenio Barba, *Theatre – Solitude, Craft, Revolt* (Aberystwyth: Black Mountain Press, 1999), pp. 71–73.

28 Photographs
A gallery of characters

Roberta Carreri in *Come! And the Day Will Be Ours*.

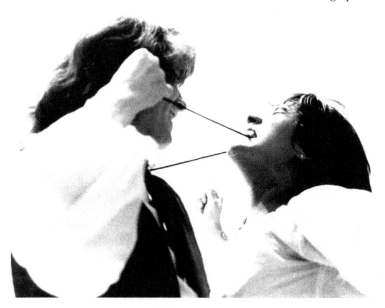

Torgeir Wethal and Roberta Carreri in *Come! And the Day Will Be Ours.*

Roberta Carreri and Else Marie Laukvik in *Come! And the Day Will Be Ours.*

Roberta Carreri, Francis Pardeilhan, Toni Cots and Iben Nagel Rasmussen in *The Million*.

Roberta Carreri in *The Million*.

Roberta Carreri and Francis Pardeilhan in *The Million*.

Julia Varley, Francis Pardeilhan, Tage Larsen and Roberta Carreri in *Brecht's Ashes*.

Roberta Carreri and Francis Pardeilhan in *Brecht's Ashes*.

Roberta Carreri in *Brecht's Ashes*.

Roberta Carreri in *The Gospel According to Oxyrhincus*.

Roberta Carreri in *Judith*.

Roberta Carreri in *Judith*.

Roberta Carreri in *Judith*.

Roberta Carreri and Kai Bredholt in *Kaosmos*.

Tina Nielsen, Roberta Carreri, Kai Bredholt and Isabel Ubeda in *Kaosmos*.

Tage Larsen, Kai Bredholt, Roberta Carreri and Julia Varley in *Ode to Progress*.

Roberta Carreri and Kai Bredholt in *Mythos*.

Roberta Carreri, Kai Bredholt and Torgeir Wethal in *Mythos*.

Roberta Carreri in *Mythos*.

Jan Ferslev and Roberta Carreri in *Salt*.

Roberta Carreri in *Salt*.

Jan Ferslev and Roberta Carreri in *Salt*.

178   *The story and the training*

Roberta Carreri in *Andersen's Dream*.

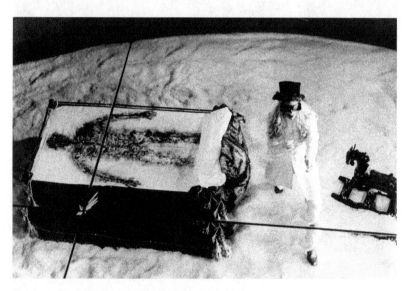

Roberta Carreri in *Andersen's Dream*.

Roberta Carreri in *The Chronic Life*.

Part II
The workshop

29 'The Dance of Intentions'

> In the Torah the Hebrew 'to know', often used in a sexual context, is not about facts but about connections. Knowledge, not as accumulation but as charge and discharge. A release of energy from one site to another.
>
> *Jeanette Winterson*

This chapter is a descriptive account of my workshop 'The Dance of Intentions', which is a sequence of physical and vocal exercises I have developed over the course of many years of teaching. The structure of the workshop is fixed, but each time I lead it something always changes because every workshop is the result of my encounter with specific individuals at a specific moment in my pedagogical trajectory.

By definition, training deals with the initial stages of apprenticeship. From the moment I learned how to learn, I have dedicated myself to enriching my training by introducing variations and exploring new techniques. The period of my daily training lasted fourteen years (from 1974 to 1988), after which my focus shifted from personal work to teaching others how to train. Even though I started to lead workshops early on, it was only in the late 1980s that I developed my research on training by means of a pedagogical practice which began to grow through teaching. Until then, I simply taught students the principles and exercises that formed part of my personal training. From that moment onwards I started to research new principles with students in my workshops.

There have been moments in the course of my pedagogical development where I have discovered 'key' principles which I used effectively for years and years, up to the point where I became bored of hearing my voice always giving the same instructions. I found ways out of this impasse by continuing to work with students, facing new situations.

The pedagogical work can continue to 'function', but in order to remain alive, to continue to be a true transmission of knowledge, it cannot limit itself to the mere repetition of recipes; it has to offer the possibility of research even for the teacher.

'The Dance of Intentions' owes its origins to a four-month workshop which I held at Odin Teatret in 1989. Today its duration varies from three days to five days. If I am performing in the evening, I only teach three hours a day; otherwise, we work for a daily maximum of five hours. In the former case we pause for ten minutes after the first two hours; in the latter case I add a break of twenty minutes after three hours.

There is also a two- or three-week version of 'The Dance of Intentions' in which I work with participants on a montage in the afternoons. This kind of work is usually held in our theatre in Holstebro.

It is important for me to work continuously, without breaks that would lead to a loss of energy. In fact, an essential part of my training consists of maintaining a specific quality of presence for a long time. My training is not very tiring from a physical point of view, but it requires a great deal of concentration.

Introduction

I always begin standing in a circle with the participants. Each one says their name and I repeat it. Memorising their names enables me to coach them individually with specific instructions. I then give this introduction:

The title of this workshop is 'The Dance of Intentions.' I will never ask you to do movements, only actions. Unlike a movement, every action has the intention of changing something. The intention emerges as an answer to a stimulus that can be felt by our bodies (hunger, an itch, pain), or by our minds (a sudden thought), or it could be provoked by something that happens around us (a sound, a call, the presence of another body, an obstacle). That is why every action is in fact a re-action. On stage, it is not enough to know what to do and how to do it; you also need to fully inhabit the action so that it does not become mechanical. You need to keep the dance of intentions alive at the base of every action, just like the way that two tango dancers who have fully embodied the steps dance in the here and now with their partner.

Exercise for the feet

We begin with a little exercise which I learnt from Torgeir Wethal on how to jump silently. Look at a point on the wall in front of you and:

1 touch the floor with the tip of your right big toe
2 roll onto the ball of your right foot
3 lift your left foot from the floor, balancing on the ball and toes of your right foot
4 slowly lower your right heel, imagining that you are squashing an orange, until you touch the floor

At this point:

1 touch the floor with the tip of your left big toe
2 roll onto the ball of your left foot
3 lift your right foot, balancing on the ball and toes of your left foot
4 imagine squashing an orange as you slowly lower your left heel until you touch the floor

Alternate the feet in a slow walk on the spot. If you wish, you can move forward or backward.

This exercise is useful for exercising the muscles of the feet.

With these three different parts of the feet in mind, now jump in the air on the spot. When you land, you should have the distinct feeling of touching the floor with the tip of your big toes, the balls of your feet and then the heels, in quick succession. The legs bend, involving the ankles, knees, and hips. In this way you will land silently. You will jump in this way when I clap my hands in the following exercise.

The Awakening

The first exercise of 'The Dance of Intentions' is seemingly quite simple, but it demands total commitment from you.

Line up next to each other, with your backs a step away from the wall.

Stop!

Do not enter the line haphazardly by forcing yourself in between two people near the centre. Accustom yourself to using your eyes: see where there is a gap and go in that direction. Create a perfect row; all of you should be on the same line.

The space you see in front of you is a raft. 'Board' it one at a time. Move in one direction and then, without stopping, change direction. The moment you stop is the signal for the next person to enter the space. It is important that you stop in a precise way, without any hesitation. For example, you can head toward the centre of the space and then, changing direction, arrive at a spot close to your point of departure. If the first person stops on the right-hand side of the space, the second should stop at a point on the other side to keep the raft in balance. Use your eyes to see the space and decide where you want to go. When all of you have 'boarded', the whole raft should be occupied evenly.

When you step into the space, avoid tensing the nape of the neck as usually happens in moments of insecurity. Your one task is to choose the point where you will stop. This demands that you truly see the space and decide accordingly. Your eyes may be open, but if you do not look actively, you will not see.

You should not walk in an artificial way, and be careful not to pick up the rhythm of the walk of the person who preceded you. You can start by walking quickly and then slow down, or do the opposite. The important thing is to vary the speed in order to avoid switching on your 'automatic pilot'.

When you walk, I do not want to hear the sound of your 'dead weight'; that is what I call the sound of a sack of skin full of bones, flesh, fat and liquids hitting the floor.

When you are standing in line, with your backs to the wall, look at a point on the wall in front of you. You should be able to see all the others in the row with your peripheral vision. Just like at night we can see things from the corners of our eyes that flee from sight the instant we look at them.

Now open your mind, your eyes, your ears, your heart, and listen with all your body.

Stop wanting to do. Fill yourself with silence. Focus only on seeing and perceiving the others in the line. The silence inside you is not a passive silence. You should not think: 'I will be the last to enter'. You will enter the space one at a time, but we do not know the order; that is the challenge.

It will only take one of you to lower their level of attention for two persons to enter the space simultaneously. If two participants set off at the same time, the next person enters the space only when the last of the two stops.

You should not aim to accomplish an act of will, but rather to react to a specific event: the person who stops. In other words, you do not have to decide when to enter, but be decided. It is only if you succeed in keeping this kind of concentration that the 'miracle' of many persons entering the space one at a time without premeditation can be accomplished. I have seen it happen before, so I know that it is possible.

When the last person stops, they squat, and all the others, using their peripheral vision, will do the same.
I will snap my fingers as a signal to start entering the space.
Ready?

At this point I allow the students a couple of seconds for my instructions to sink in and to obtain the necessary silence for the exercise. Then I snap my fingers.

They enter the space one by one. If two participants set off at the same time, the next person enters the space only when the last of the two have stopped. When all of them are squatting I say:

Now you are all squatting. This is not a rest position, but a state of being alert which allows you to react to an impulse at any moment by jumping.

When I clap my hands, you will all jump, turn in the air, and land in a squat without putting your hands on the floor, facing a different direction.

Over time I no longer give the signal to jump. When one jumps, the rest do so simultaneously. This is a way of keeping them present: ready to react to an impulse from a companion, but also to decide to jump and pull the others along. The leader is the one who thinks of the others and guides them.

Now listen to the silence of the room, to the various sounds, near and far away, that enter the space.

I clap my hands – they jump, turn in the air and land in a squat.

Look around and see the space around you.

I clap my hands – once or three times in succession, they jump, turn in the air and land in a squat.

Close your eyes: how many lamps are there in this room? This is a real question, keep your eyes closed and reply.

Various answers.

You can now open your eyes.

Observe how the nape of your neck moves now that you are not just looking but truly seeing with your eyes. First, you were simply fixing your eyes in front of you, believing that you were seeing. In reality the eyes are just the windows to the world; the action of seeing takes place in the brain.

I clap my hands – they jump, turn in the air and land in a squat.

When you land, remember that I do not want to hear the sound of a 'sack of skin' falling on the floor. Withhold the weight. Land silently, making use of the joints and muscles of your feet to cushion the impact with the floor.

I clap my hands twice – they jump, turn in the air and land in a squat.

You have to react immediately to the sound of my hands. Your legs are already in *sats*,[1] you only have to 'release the spring'. It is the tip of your head that guides you upwards. Do the action of observing the colour of the floor, the cracks in the walls, the hanging lamps, while listening to the sounds in the room. At the same time, be ready to react, with a jump, to the clap of my hands. You have to be completely focused and open at the same time. This is only possible if you manage to keep any other thought from your minds.

I clap my hands – they jump, turn in the air and land in a squat.

And now do the action of standing.

They stand up. I clap my hands – they jump, turn in the air and land standing up.

Exactly: when I clap my hands you should jump and turn in the air, just like you were doing when you were squatting, but you now land standing, facing a different direction.

I clap my hands – they jump.

Stop! Your knees bend when you land. Keep them bent, do not straighten them because otherwise you lose the necessary *sats* to jump.

I clap my hands – they jump.

Avoid making any noise when you land. Imagine stopping two centimetres above the floor.

I clap my hands – they jump.

Run.
Stop.
Run.
Stop.

I clap my hands – they jump.
I clap my hands – they jump.

You are now in *sats* position. Your legs are ready to jump or run because you do not know which instruction I will give. Remember this feeling.

The Snake

The experience of working with masters of Japanese theatre and dance has led me to discover my internal axis, what I call the *snake*. This is an invisible muscle that every actor uses consciously or instinctively to amplify their presence on stage. The *snake* starts in the eyes, which are its 'head'. It then runs down parallel to, and on the inner side of, the spinal column. The *snake* is not the spinal column, but rather an invisible muscle that runs alongside it.

Some of you have your knees fully extended, locked. Everybody should lock their knees like them. Try to dance with the tail of the *snake*. It is difficult, right?

Now bend your knees slightly and try again to dance with the tail of your *snake*. Can you feel the difference? The energy now flows freely. That is why when we work with the *snake* we should not have our knees fully extended (or locked, like those of a horse sleeping on its feet).

Try to dance with your spinal column.

They dance.

I only see backs that are moving freely. You are not feeling any resistance, and I only see movements.

Now dance with your *snake* instead.

Try to remember a summer day when you stood up to your shoulders in the sea; the sun was shining and the water was clear. You playfully moved your arms in the sea, left and right under the surface of the water. If your feet were not planted firmly on the sea bed, you probably lost your balance and fell. Then you stood up again, this time with your legs wide apart, and began again to move your arms, making the water run through your fingers. Contrary to the first time, the action now started from your hips; it was not just the arms which were engaged, but the body as a whole.

Now do this action.

They do it.

Repeat it without using your arms – just the torso, the nape of the neck and the head.

They do it.

The strength that you now feel in your back comes from the *snake*.

Your gaze is the tongue of the *snake* and as such it flicks in and out. When it goes out, your gaze becomes strong; when it retreats, it becomes softer.

I will now put on some music and I want you to dance with your *snake* only. Snakes do not have legs, arms or shoulders, so do not dance with them. Your feet have to be firmly planted on the floor, as if they were suction cups. Remember to dance with the tail, the belly, the torso, the nape of the neck and the tongue of the *snake*, in different directions.

I put on some music and they dance in place until I turn the volume up and say 'Fill the space!' and they allow themselves to be drawn by the impulse of the snake, moving in the space, filling it.

Then I say 'On the spot', and they keep dancing with their feet planted on the floor.

'Slowly', and the dance slows down considerably.

'Big' or 'Small', and they change the size.

They keep dancing, following my instructions, changing the size, speed, intensity and direction till the end of the music.

Cobra

The *snake* can transform into a *cobra*. What distinguishes the cobra from other snakes is its ability to rise on its coils into a vertical position.

To transform your *snake* into a *cobra* place your feet parallel to each other and:

1. bend your knees slightly and tuck in your tailbone while drawing your navel toward your spine. You need to engage your abdominal muscles to do this, as if you want to sit down.
2. lengthen the nape of your neck by lowering your chin. Be careful not to thrust your head forward. Rather, lightly press your head backward by pulling in your chin.
3. intensify your gaze by contracting your abdominal muscles and keeping your gaze fixed on the same point in front of you in spite of the fact that your chin is lowered.

The result is a 'flat' back, like an ironing board, with your centre of gravity right between your heels. With your axis completely vertical, maintain your equilibrium on the rear part of the feet. Do not use too much strength because in doing so you create negative tensions that block the flow of energy.

By adopting this position you achieve a form of dynamic immobility.

You do not look particularly friendly. This is not because you are thinking about something unpleasant.

The normal position of the gaze in relation to the face is that of ninety degrees; the face follows your eyes if you look upwards or downwards. Now keep your eyes fixed on a point in front of you – do not change it, even if you lower your chin and elongate the nape of your neck. In this way, the face/eyes relation changes and causes a small internal tension, giving the impression of aggression.

Now adopt the *cobra* position following the three phases I just described. One. Two. Three.

When I say 'now':

- transfer weight onto the right foot;
- slide your left foot towards the right and then slide it forward until it moves beyond the right foot;
- transfer weight onto the left foot;
- slide your right foot forward keeping your weight on the left foot;
- transfer weight onto the right foot.

In this way you can move forward while maintaining the *cobra* position. Be careful not to lose it. Your pelvis stays slightly tucked with your navel drawn toward your spine. The nape of your neck is stretched, the chin lowered. Your axis needs to be as straight as a spindle. I do not want to see any 'duck butts', which appear when abdominal muscles are relaxed.

This position is the result of a complex architecture of small internal tensions (*in-tensions*) that produce a feeling of strength and power. The legs and arms remain free from tension.

Cobra with resistance

Pair up. Find a partner who is more or less your height. Stand in front of each other, the one in front with their back to the other. When I say 'one', 'two', 'three' adopt the *cobra* position. The person in the back puts their fingertips on the hip-bones of the person in front. It is important that you do not lower your head to look at the feet. Instead, fix your eyes on the head of your companion and use your peripheral vision.

When I say 'now', transfer your weight onto one foot and slide the other one forward. The moment the person in front transfers their weight is important, because it communicates to the person behind which foot will move first. Move forward with the person behind applying light pressure to their partner's hip-bones, thus providing them with a little resistance.

Now.

It is important that both partners keep their *cobras* in a vertical position. The person in the back needs to stay very close to avoid bending forward in an attempt to keep their hands on their partner's hips, while being careful not to tread on their heels.

When you reach the other end of the room, stop but maintain your *cobra* positions. The person in the back removes their hands from their partner's hip-bones.

Cross one foot in front of the other and turn in place, making sure you do not rise onto your tiptoes. You must always keep the same height (which is a little lower than your true height because your knees are slightly bent), both when you move in the space and when you turn on the spot.

The person who was in front and is now in the back places their hands on the hip-bones of their partner. Repeat the *cobra* walk, in pairs, with resistance, as before.

After you alternate three or four times, leave your partner and move separately in the space, keeping alive the physical memory of the resistance provided by your partner.

Now take a chair each.

Place the chairs in a row and sit down.
When I say 'now', adopt the *cobra* position in three stages.
Now.

They do it.

When I say 'now', stand up and move in the space.
  Now.

They do it.

Dynamic immobility

Now leave the *cobra* position and dance again with the *snake*.

When I say 'one', 'two', 'three', react to the intensity of my voice and take on again the position of the *cobra* in three phases. If my voice is strong, adopt the *cobra* position in a strong manner, if it is gentle, then gently.

Now keep your *cobra* position with gentle energy or, as I call it, 'cobra light'. When I say 'now', move swiftly around the space, occupying it fully, frequently changing direction and turning on an axis like a whirlpool to see who is behind you. Keep your *cobra* straight, do not relax the abdominals that let your stomach and bottom stick out. Remember that this is an active position and does not occur automatically: it is necessary to 'enact' it at all times.

Keep looking in front of you, without ever turning your head. Use your peripheral vision to see what is on both sides.

When I say 'stop!' freeze the action. Your body is completely immobile, while your mind continues to run towards the point you are looking at.

When I say 'go!' change direction before you move in the space. You have to decide quickly where to go. The companions who cut in front of you are positive obstacles that oblige you to react by changing direction. Be decided. Do not follow straight lines for a long time. Cut across the centre of the space. Change direction. Do not stay in the centre. Use the whole space.

'Go!'
'Stop'.

I repeat these instructions several times.
  The objective of this exercise is to train the maintenance of dynamic immobility even for long stretches. The duration of the stops varies.

> Sometimes the stops follow each other in quick succession with brief intervals in between; sometimes the students have to keep dynamic immobility for thirty seconds or more. As soon as the concentration diminishes, it becomes apparent in the body. So I say to them: How strong is your will?

Slow motion

> *I give the following instructions as they maintain their dynamic immobility:*

When I say 'now', start to melt your *snake* from the state of *cobra*, and make a big step in slow motion. Then imagine jumping a hurdle in slow motion. In this case the moment of flight does not exist and one of the feet has to remain in contact with the floor. You can also use the image of stepping over a chair in front of you.

Your point of strength should be in the centre of your body, in the zone between the lumbar vertebra and the abdominal muscles. That is where the step originates, which is then extended to the rest of the *snake*: from the coccyx to the eyes. The step begins much earlier than when the first foot lifts from the floor. Your body moves in between two fixed points: the one you are looking at on the wall in front of you and the foot which supports you. Your body is in continuous movement between these two points.

To accomplish this kind of step you have to approach it in a different way than how you usually do in everyday life, i.e. by lifting the knee in front of you.

The leg that initiates the step first moves backwards (rather than forward as happens instinctively); raise the knee out to the side, and then, moving the leg forward, step over the imaginary chair. At this point, if you transfer your weight onto this leg as we do in everyday life you will lose balance and fall forward, interrupting the flow of your slow motion. To this end, you have to keep the weight on the rear leg and both legs must bend together to complete the step.

The arms are also part of the step as they help to keep your balance.

Have the feeling of breathing with all your body to avoid creating tension. You might begin to lose your balance and react by tensing the hands, shoulders, legs or feet. These instinctive tensions will make it even more difficult to stay in balance.

> *They do it.*

I can see that you do not have any resistance when you take your steps. You have to imagine that you are walking on the bottom of the sea. At that depth the water envelops you entirely, creating resistance, but it is not solid. Remember the feeling you had when you were in the sea with the water up to your shoulders and you moved your arms left and right under the surface of the water with your feet firmly planted on the seabed. The water resisted you. It is this kind of resistance that we want to evoke to avoid creating any tension: real but gentle. As you take the step you have to imagine that you are pushing gently with your cheek, forehead, arms, hands, legs, feet, with the water all around you.

They do it. Sometimes I put on some slow music to accompany their work.

Now find three ways of sitting down in slow motion without touching the floor with your hands. The moment your bottom touches the floor is the signal to start rising up again.

You probably cannot apply the same logic you do in everyday life in order to sit down or stand up in slow motion. You need to find other ways, thinking with the body in a different manner. Focus on the architecture of your body, listen to it. These two actions are accomplished by means of a continuous transference of weight from one part of the body to the other. When you sit down or stand up, it helps if you imagine two points in your body that pull in opposite directions. Now that you are on 'planet slow motion', everything that you do, even if it is brushing your hair back from your face or blowing your nose, needs to be done in slow motion. It is important not to interrupt the *flow*.

They do it.

I will now ask you to create a sequence of 'three deaths and resurrections' in slow motion. Imagine being fatally hit at a point in your body and falling in slow motion until you lie down on the floor. Then stand up again, starting from an impulse in a precise part of the body. Each time change the point where you were hit, the manner in which you lie down, and the location of the impulse that lifts you up again.

They do it.

You can now perform a sequence of fixed actions, or physical exercises like backward or forward rolls, head or shoulder stands, bridges that start while standing up or kneeling. The important thing is to have precise tasks that allow you to keep thinking with all your body, in slow motion.

They do it.

Seaweed

Come to standing with your feet parallel to each other. Keeping the *flow* of slow motion within you, think that you are seaweed. Imagine that a big fish passes in front of you, and then a small fish to your right. You react 'passively' to the fish around you: it is the water that moves you. The water can be very calm, like the Sargasso Sea, or it can have intersecting currents of varying speeds. Imagine fish that lightly brush against you at different heights.

They do it.

Flexing the eyes

Forget the image of seaweed and choose a spot on the wall in front of you, about ten centimetres above eye level.

Burn that spot with your gaze.

Without letting go of that spot, show me with your finger the part of your body which is the most energised. Exactly, it is the abdomen. Slowly let go of the spot, pulling back your gaze until it seems like you are observing the internal surface of the pupils of your eyes. Retrace the path until you touch the spot on the wall again. Burn it! Pull back your gaze, making sure you do not lower your eyelids, until you reach the surface of your eyes.

Now start to look backwards until you let your gaze fall inside you.

Relax your cheeks, forehead, chin, tongue, ears and nose. Drop the mask, the *persona* you show the world. Let your gaze re-emerge slowly to the surface of your eyes and then out in the space until it touches the spot you have chosen and burn it! Leave it and pull back your gaze until it reaches the surface of your eyes and then let it drop inside you. The muscles that support the eyes are completely relaxed, like all the other muscles in the face.

You are in a glass bell. Nothing can touch you. Nothing can hurt you. You are safe in there. The silence is perfect and sweet. Turn your head to the right and then to the left, keeping the gaze inside you. Our eyes are programmed to constantly focus on the images in front of us. To avoid these small automatic adjustments of the eyes, you have to keep your gaze unfocused within the glass bell. Sit and stand in slow motion keeping this unfocused gaze, and then let your gaze emerge again until it reaches and touches the spot on the wall. Burn it!

This exercise, which I call 'flexing the eyes', is repeated several times. It is not easy to teach the eyes to do the action of 'not seeing'. The idea is to use the eyes to create the impression of absence or presence in another dimension. Like the eyes of Marlon Brando when he dies in Mutiny on the Bounty, *or Al Pacino in* Scent of a Woman. *The eyes are an essential part of the actor's body. When we look at someone (on stage or in life), we look at their eyes. We send a precise message when we avoid someone's eyes. That is why it is important to make the most of the potential of our gaze.*

To enable students to feel concretely the change in the 'fire' of their eyes, I ask them to do the following exercise.

Form two rows, facing each other, four metres apart. You are Row A and Row B. Every participant should have someone more or less their height in front of them. Row A will lift the index and middle fingers on their right hand until they reach the level of their partners' eyes in Row B, who will then 'burn them' with their gaze. Using peripheral vision, Row A will then move forward together. Row B will relax their gaze as the fingers gradually move closer, until they are two centimetres away from their eyes. At this point, Row A lowers their arms while Row B will try to maintain their gaze as it is, without allowing the eyes to focus. This is the most difficult thing to accomplish. Row A will again lift their fingers to a point two centimetres away from their partner's eyes, and using their peripheral vision they will walk backwards together. When Row A reaches their point of departure, they lower their right arms. Row B will then lift the index and middle fingers of their right hands until they reach the eye level of their partners in Row A. Now do the exercise again, changing roles.

They do it several times.

Leading points

I discovered this principle thanks to a question that an Odin Week Festival participant once asked me. After a week of workshops, demonstrations and performances, he asked me: 'I want to create my own personal training, do you have any advice for me?' I would have liked to answer: 'For this whole week at Odin we haven't done anything but provide you with suggestions on how to create your own training!' Instead I said: 'The important thing is to take the first step.' And I left. His question irritated me because it showed that he did not get the point of our efforts, which was precisely to inspire one's own work. However, I felt some remorse for my curt reply. So I decided to put into practice the advice I gave him, as if a master had given it to me. I stood up in order to take the first step. Keeping the axis of my body straight, perfectly vertical from my heels to the top of my head, I began to move forward starting from the tip of my forehead at the roots of my hair. I realised that by following my weight I could accomplish the step starting from the head. Once again, starting completely upright, I moved my shoulders forward and following them I made a step. Pursuing this logic I found that a step can start from other parts of the body: the heart, hips, knees, toes, heels, elbows and wrists.

At the start of the step it is important to keep the centre of gravity between the feet. To illustrate this position I use the idea of the anaconda, *the longest snake in the world. I have the feeling that this snake starts from the heels and goes all the way up to the top of the head. The knees are not bent, but nor are they locked. Another way of achieving this position is to imagine that you are two centimetres taller than you actually are. Also for this snake, the abdominal muscles have to be contracted and the chin slightly lowered – just like we did when we were children and our parents measured our height by placing us next to a doorframe and making a horizontal line next to a date. We grew half a centimetre by lowering the chin.*

Adopt the *anaconda* position: with heels firmly planted on the floor and chin slightly lowered, imagine growing two centimetres taller than your actual height. Keeping this *light internal tension*, shift your weight starting from the point where your forehead meets your hairline. Imagine that an invisible horse is pulling you from that point. When you are about to lose balance, move swiftly a foot forward, thus accomplishing the first step. Be careful not to land heavily. The impulse (the pull of the invisible cable) is renewed for every step. Change directions: forward, sideways, backward. The head leads by moving in one direction, followed by the rest of the body, ending with the feet which make a step in that direction. This kind of step is interesting because it is the result of a micro drama: the head wants to go forward while the feet want to stay where they are until the last moment. There comes a moment in this little conflict where you 'have' to take the step in order not to fall, thus making a true action. Do not let go of your weight, falling into the next step, but keep it always in control. The step happens exactly at the instant before you lose balance, and you can be taken forward, sideways or backward. Be careful not to jut your chin forward, thus breaking the line of the nape of your neck. If this happens, I will see a body that wants to show me that the head is leading. This is not the objective of this principle. The logic that guides you to make a step is an internal one and concerns your way of thinking with the body. The result has to be natural, not artificial. The logic should manifest itself through a formalised presence, not as an illustration of the leading point.

Now try to start from the shoulders. The invisible cable pulls you forward, backward, towards one side and the other. If one shoulder is pulled forward and the other backward, you end up turning on the spot. You should never lift your shoulders. Pay particular attention when changing direction from forward to backward because, especially in those of you who have practised the 'plastique exercises', there is the tendency to lift the shoulders in a rolling movement when changing directions. This should be avoided because it gives a sense of artificiality.

Standing still with your *anaconda* stretched upwards, try to let your heart (the centre of your chest) be pulled forward – backward – to the left – to the right. Then forward and left simultaneously (i.e. you turn) – forward and right – backward and right – backwards and left. Now do the same and let the invisible cable pull you in the space, compelling you to take one step or more in various directions. For example, by moving forward and to the right, the heart turns you in that direction.

Now it is the hips' turn. The invisible cable is attached to your hip bones and pulls you in different directions. Make sure that you do not break the verticality of your axis. If one hip is shifted forward and the other backward, you will find yourself turning on the spot.

Do not stick your belly out when moving forward. Engaging the muscles of your buttocks can help to avoid this. When the hip bones pull you backward, refrain from sticking your bottom out. In this case, it can help to imagine that the navel draws in towards the spinal column.

When the step starts from the knee it moves forward, not upward. Lift the foot from the floor to make a step, but not in 'marching' style. When the knee drags you backward, you are pulled from the rear part of the knee, resulting, in this case, in fully extended knees. Like the other *leading points*, steps initiated from the knees can be accomplished in different directions.

When the tips of the feet lead they move forward, almost brushing against the floor. This is reminiscent of ballet dancers walking off-stage. When the tip of the foot moves backward, it is the tip of the big toe that should lead the body. Everyone has an innate fear of bumping their big toes. In order to protect them, we tend to instinctively touch the floor with the fleshy part of the toes first, as we do in everyday life.

The result is that the most backward part of the body will be the heel instead of the big toe, thus removing from the exercise that element of danger which forces us to be precise and thereby ignites our presence. The tips of the feet can also move sideways.

Heels: when you move forward, the heels cannot be the parts that lead the body. However, by using the mental image of the invisible cable pulling the heel forward, your walk will take on a distinctive character, without being artificial. If the heels move backwards, the result is exactly the same as when you walk backwards in daily life. Like the other *leading points*, the heels can move sideways and make you change direction – for example, by crossing one leg behind the other.

Elbows: forward, backward, sideways. When the inner sides of the elbows lead be careful not to lift them too much, otherwise it will be impossible for you to follow them unless you can walk up walls. The impulse is tiny but it has to be precise; the pull of the invisible cable is light. Be careful not to fall forward. Elbows can move backward or sideways. One elbow forward and the other backward, and you turn.

Wrists: everything I said about the elbows also applies to the wrists. The pull of the invisible cable is light and care must be taken not to lift the wrist too much, so that we avoid pointing upwards rather than directly forward. Both the inner and outer parts of the wrists can pull you either forward or backward. One wrist forward and the other backward, and you end up turning.

Now adopt the *anaconda* position and find your inner silence. Wait until the first *leading point* moves and leads you to make the first step. From now onwards your feet will no longer be in the position of their point of departure (parallel and next to each other) because a new *leading point* will make you change direction, surprising you in the flow of successive steps. You move, letting various *leading points* alternate and take you in different directions in the space. Your steps can be big or small, quick or slow, strong or gentle. Do not switch on the 'automatic pilot': decide, vary. The degree of intensity is manifested in the intensity of your gaze.

After exploring this principle for some days, you can work on two *leading points* simultaneously. For example, the head wants to go forward and the heels backward. Who wins? The *in-tension* that arises from this micro drama can be used to exemplify a situation of indecision.

Work with the *leading points*, sometimes amplifying them to the maximum, at other times minimising them. Remember that you are two centimetres taller than you actually are – extend the *anaconda*.

Say aloud a text which you know by heart. Avoid interpreting it. Allow the text to adapt to the dynamics of the minimised *leading points*. The criteria that you follow should not be made evident to the audience. It is a logic that supports the text, making it coherent, like the gestures that accompany our speech in everyday life, only in this case we do it consciously and in a formalised manner.

Start with one *leading point* at a time. Do not change the *leading point* with every word. Try to give to your text the flow of your actions' directions and intensities. Imagine that you are addressing the spectators around you.

After exploring various possibilities, compose a sequence of *leading points* to accompany the text. Repeat this various times until you learn it by heart.

Now find a partner and have a dialogue: alternate by saying a phrase each, using the score of your *leading points*.

Take an object (for example, a notebook, a bottle, a shawl) and create a sequence of actions using *leading points* which justify the presence of the object in your hands. What do you want to do with it? To whom do you want to give it? Why? Learn the sequence.

Find a partner and have a dialogue using the actions with objects.

> *During my workshops I sometimes meet students who have explored something very similar to this principle when working with students of Michael Chekhov. I was not aware of his work on this aspect, nor of the work he developed on the various qualities of energy.*
>
> *With the passing of time I have realised that when researching in depth, one discovers principles that recur in different contexts. Just like the way that in the Andes one can come across socks and jumpers with patterns similar to those found in Norway.*
>
> *If done properly, keeping the image of the* anaconda *and imagining being two centimetres taller, the* leading points *can strike a chord within us that reawaken feelings and emotions. The resonance of such chords can in turn affect and strike chords in spectators, moving them. For instance, the head* leading point *evokes menace. The heart* leading point *while moving forward: openness and optimism. The heart* leading point *while moving backwards: sadness. The hips while moving forward: sensuality. Forward-facing wrists: vulnerability. And so on. It is not that I think of something which evokes these feelings in me; it is the active position of the body that awakens them.*

I can use leading points *to compose scenes for the director to work with, or to emphasise a text. Gesture is part of language, confirming or contradicting the* semantic meaning of words. Used in an almost concealed way, leading points can give life to a text and help us avoid everyday gesticulation.

Actions with hands and feet

The following principle was inspired by a work session led by Claire Heggen of Théâtre du Mouvement, which I observed at Odin Teatret. I put some music on and invite participants to dance freely around the space.

Keep moving in the space and simply repeat the actions that I do with my arms and hands:

- *Throwing.* It is important that you perform the action with precision: it starts with a closed hand next to a hip and ends with the hand open and the arm almost fully extended sideways.

If some of the students do a movement instead of a precise action, I give them a sock or a shoe and ask them to throw it to me while paying attention to the dynamic of the action.

I teach them the following three actions, one after the other:

- *Stopping* by making 'stop' with the hands,
- *Beckoning* using the arm or just the index finger
- *Pointing*

Work with each action, exploring various sizes, intensities, directions and speeds; direct your attention to people living on the tenth floor, or to a cat passing right in front of you. Use one hand at a time or both of them at the same time.

They do it.
I show them the action of throwing something in front of me, or behind my right foot, and ask them to tell me which one is the most interesting. They always answer that it is the second.

So why do you always perform your actions in front of you? When I tell you to do actions in different directions, I am not only referring to the space, but also in relation to your body. Remember to beckon, point, stop and throw, even to persons behind you. This will help you to overcome the automatisms of everyday life, thus discovering new possibilities.

Explore these actions one after the other, and then alternate between using them as actions and reactions.

These actions can also be performed 'in rewind', transforming them into other actions. For example, the action of 'throwing' becomes 'grasping'. By changing their size, intensity and speed, actions take on different meanings and become other actions. This is what I call the metamorphoses of actions.

The same process applies to these five actions with the feet:

- The *Wheel*, where you put the heel first on the floor and roll down on through the rest of the foot, imagining it going round like a wheel. The tip of the big toe disconnects from the floor only after the other heel touches the floor; in this way the contact with the floor is continuous. If you walk quickly, maintaining the *anaconda* upright, you can change direction simply by shifting your weight from one side of the body to the other, as when riding a motorcycle.
- *Kicking Sand with the Feet*, as we enjoy doing on the beach, flicking with the tip of the toes.
- Touching a *Slug* with the toes and reacting by lifting the foot in disgust. The action of lifting the foot should not start from the knee but from the contraction of your abdominal muscles, as happens when we are disgusted by something.
- Saying *Enough* by sliding a foot sideways and opening the arms with the hands parallel to the floor. Stop the action sharply, with determination.
- *Crushing* a cigarette butt under your toes with a semi-rotating movement.

Explore these actions, first individually by changing the size, intensity, direction and speed, just as we did with the arms and hands, and then alternate them, using them as reactions.

All these actions with the feet can be performed in rewind while moving backwards. Explore each action, varying size, intensity, direction and speed.

They do it.

Now move through all the actions, using those of both the hands and the feet, alternating and changing them. You can change them, making them very big or very small, changing speed and intensity. These actions can be used to accompany a text that you know by heart.

As with *leading points*, it is important that the gesture is not artificial. It is also important that the actions are minimised so that the attention of the spectator is not distracted from the meaning of the text. When the text is important, the actions that inform it need to be reduced. It is crucial to remain faithful to the intention of the action. Sometimes it is enough to think it with the body while saying the text. The important thing is not to transform the action into a movement by removing the essence: the intention, which is located in the *snake*. Remember that the *snake* is the seat of intentions and that your eyes are the head of the *snake*. The gaze is an essential part of the action.

Jumps

> *The participants form a circle. I ask them individually to invent a jump, which the others repeat immediately. In this way they all learn a repeatable sequence of jumps in a couple of minutes. Then I put on some rhythmic music and ask them to form a row standing side by side. I have them move forward together, performing the jump sequence, following the rhythm of the music. Once again, they need to use their peripheral vision to move in unison. They are compelled to think about what they are doing, in addition to timing their actions with those of their companions. That is: being in what they are doing while simultaneously being open to what is happening around them.*

Looking with the snake

Take a chair. Sit down. Lengthen your *snake*, and from this position do the action of looking around you, in different directions. Create a triangle of oppositions: tail, chest, head. The tail goes to the right, the chest to the left and the head to the right. Or: the tail goes backward, the chest forward, the head backward. Explore various combinations. As with *leading points*, you will find that certain combinations will awake in you different states of being.

Pushing and pulling

After years of work, I have come to the conclusion that every action is the result of a composition of two fundamental actions: pushing and pulling. For example, if I want to pick up a glass of water, my fingers press around the glass while my arm pulls towards my mouth. Let us explore these two actions.

In pairs, put the palms of your hands against your companion's. Explore the action of pushing, starting from your *snake*. Be careful not to lean your dead weight on your partner. If this happens, your *snake* will not be active and the action can never become a physical memory.

Move around the space, lowering yourself or lifting up on your toes while doing the action of pushing. Avoid always mirroring your partner's actions; work also in opposition to them. For example, if your partner stands up, you lower yourself. Avoid lying down on the floor because this impedes your *snake*.

How light can the action of pushing be? How strong? Remember that this is not Greco-Roman wrestling, but an exploration of pushing with a partner. Listen to your partner.

They do it.

Now entwine your fingers with those of your companion and explore the action of pulling. Make sure that you do not lean backward. The action has to be real and you should feel the change in the muscular tone of your back. Explore the action of pulling like you did with pushing. Avoid staying in the same spot. Move around the space while doing the action. Use your peripheral vision to avoid bumping into other pairs. You have to be in the action you are doing, listen to your partner's intention and see the space around you.

In your pairs, create four sequences of three actions each. For example: push pull push – stop – pull push pull – stop – push pull push – stop – pull push pull. The moments of stop are moments of dynamic immobility, what I call 'statues'. Alternate and vary the intensity, direction, size and speed. These sequences of actions will lead you to move in the space. Fix these sequences as well as the steps that take you around the space.

Now that you have memorised a sequence of fixed actions, perform it with your hands at a distance of ten centimetres from your partner's palms, but keep the same intensity you had before while doing the actions of pulling and pushing.

After performing the sequence in this way a few times, leave your partner and in another part of the space, repeat the sequence of actions on your own.

Reducing the actions

Now that you have a sequence of fixed actions, a score, you can perform it in different ways. For example, without using the arms – in this way you realise that the action occurs mainly in the *snake* and that holding the arms in another position changes the meaning of the action.

Now do your sequence:

- At 50%. That is, all actions have to be held back. If at the start your arms were next to the thighs and you lifted them simultaneously until your hands arrived in front of your chest in order to meet your partner's hands, now they will accomplish just half of that trajectory, thus stopping at the belly and closer to the body, while the palms of your hands will not be vertical but leaning downwards at an angle of forty-five degrees. Every action is held back, but the same intention is maintained.
- At 20%. This is less than the half of the 50%.
- And then 1%. In this case you do the sequence only with the *snake*, almost without moving.

Now perform the sequence of actions, alternating between 100%, 50%, 20% and 1%.

Different qualities of energy

You can repeat the same sequence of actions with different qualities of energy – what I call 'water states'. Let us explore each of them, repeating the sequence a few times:

- *Fog.* Your *snake* is fog, your eyes are fog. Is fog hard or soft? What colour is it?
- *A stream* that flows from a mountain. It is quick but slows down suddenly when it comes across a flat stretch.
- *The Amazon river.* Wide and powerful, it carries along with it carcasses of animals and trunks of dead trees.
- *Bubbles of mineral water,* or champagne, that rise from the bottom of the glass and burst on the nose. Tiny and light.
- *The sea during a storm,* when enormous waves rise and smash against the shore, overwhelming and carrying everything with them.
- *The water of a lake at night.* Black and seemingly tranquil, its dark surface calm and clear.
- *Iceberg,* which moves slowly and majestically. Hard and cold.

Improvise by alternating freely between these different qualities of energy while performing your sequence. Explore all possibilities.

Do not switch on the 'automatic pilot'. Be decisive and choose the next quality of energy. In this way you become accustomed to thinking with the body, keeping your concentration alive.

Now you can reduce the sequence to 50%, 20% or 1% while you are working with the different qualities of energy. In this way you explore all the possibilities of your sequence, moving freely from a kind a dance to a form of dynamic immobility.

You can use these different kinds of energy also in your vocal training.

Conclusion

This sequence of principles has changed over the years, and it will continue to change. But this is what I am teaching today.

What you have learnt is now yours. However, in order to achieve results you need to allow yourself the time to work. An essential element of training is continuity. You need to confront, on a daily or at least a regular basis, principles which initially require your total concentration. Then, once they are learnt and assimilated, they need constant attention to be kept alive.

Training helps us to face our motivation on a daily basis, reaffirming our need to do what we do. It also teaches us how to keep a score of actions alive. This is exactly what is required of us when playing the same role night after night, when our work risks becoming mechanical.

Each one of you will interpret my words according to your experience, your personal story. The important thing is to have a point of departure. What you make of this, how you develop the work on these principles, will depend on your personal motivation.

Note

1   *Sats* is the Norwegian word for 'impulse'. To be in *sats* position allows me to react and change direction at any moment. I describe *sats* in more detail in Chapter 5.

Part III
Perspectives

30 A memory not only for and by itself

A note on methodology by Francesca Romana Rietti

> Every thought is born from experience, but no fact of experience
> has any meaning or even any consistency unless it undergoes a
> process of imagination and thought.
>
> Hannah Arendt, *The Life of the Mind*

Traces in the Snow is a work demonstration created by Roberta Carreri in 1988, which still forms an integral part of Odin Teatret's repertory. The idea of transforming it into a book, with the text and photographic documentation of the demonstration complementing each other, goes back to 2005. This is the linear origin of *Tracce: Training e storia di un'attrice dell'Odin Teatret* (Traces: The Training and Story of an Odin Teatret Actress), the first edition of the book in Italian. However, for me there is another logic at work at its roots: one that involves paradoxes.

At Odin Teatret, the term 'work demonstration' refers to a type of theatre that is halfway between a pedagogical situation and a performance. In this situation, contrary to what happens in a performance, the actor or actress reveals their technique. Showing one's personal physical and vocal training highlights and explains the principles that organise the actor's scenic presence and the organicity of their behaviour; by revealing the non-linear logic that guides the generation of performance material, it presents fragments or entire scenes. A work demonstration is a *study in action* of the principles that govern the profession and art of the actor, whose rhythm is conditioned by the continuous alternation between theory and practice. The oral exposition of theoretical knowledge and principles (the so-called text) acts as a counterpoint to their practical demonstration, and vice versa. Similar to that of a conference, the text of a work demonstration is not rigidly fixed and possesses the characteristics of spoken language. Essentially, it can correct itself, undergo variations and adaptations provoked by the context and move forward or backward, anticipating or postponing the action. This happens precisely because the words that constitute the text are inseparable, and at times even incomprehensible, from the live body that incarnates the principles, performs the actions and gives life to the images. Every time I observe *Traces in the Snow* I perceive a complementary dynamic between words and body: the body shows what the words cannot say, and in their turn, the words say what the body cannot show.

How do you restore in the solidity of the written page the liquid quality of the dialogue between text and action, word and body? Above all, how do you transfigure the words to recreate on paper a non-static analogue of the live body that acts on stage?

I think these questions have been among the challenges that nourished, perhaps secretly, the composition of this book whose author appeared to be led by this paradoxical logic: how to retain in the passage between liquid and solid state the fluidity that characterises the phenomenon of scenic presence. This involves the same logic that organises her professional work as actress and teacher, her training, as well as the creation of her characters for a performance. How do you retain, in the fixity of form, the dynamic and fluid quality of life with all its shades? Or rather, how is it possible to search, through form, the way to get rid of its fixity?

Therefore, there exists a very close rapport between the creative process that orients Robert Carreri the actress and the one which involves her intellectual systematisation of her work, which is essentially a research of those 'instrument-words' capable of transmitting the quality and necessity that guide experience. In a similar process, a decisive role is played by the ambivalent relationship that links the author of this book to words. In fact, if there is a red line that runs throughout the writing of this book, bestowing upon it a vital tension, it is precisely the coexistence of a mistrust of words (declared by the author herself in the Introduction) and the necessity of confronting that mistrust. There is not a performance or activity of Odin Teatret in which Roberta Carreri has participated about which she has not kept a diary or written notes. Is this not also another paradox that guides the writing of this author? It is as if, subterraneously, there exists in her the awareness that only the written word is capable of recreating a long-term analogue of those images that the body-mind of the actor embodies with the precise intention of making an indelible impression in the spectator's memory. Escape the ambiguity of words, yes, but through them create a memory. A memory that is not only for and by itself – private – but a memory which transmits: the written page contains the tension that does not disperse experience.

A memory not only for and by itself   213

Before reaching its definitive version, *Tracce* has been through various possible structures, many drafts, infinite deletions, corrections and revisions. Some chapters, many of which are complemented by photographs from the work demonstration, follow the text of *Traces in the Snow* quite faithfully. Other chapters have been rewritten according to a different logic and integrated with material from many sources: fragments from work diaries of performances, notes taken during various pedagogical situations, and texts extracted from edited notebooks during individual and group travels. All references to private life and the autobiographical parts that concern Roberta Carreri prior to joining Odin Teatret in 1974 are completely new as far as the work demonstration is concerned. The same holds for the three chapters on *The Gospel According to Oxyrhincus, Kaosmos* and *Salt*.[1]

As regards the initial idea of translating *Traces in the Snow* into a book, today these pages appear to me like the result of the metamorphosis experienced by the passage of words from spoken to written language, and of the dilation experienced by the body in its passage from stage to paper.

Among the many pages that have been deleted from this book there is one of which I am particularly fond. It concerns a diary fragment written by Roberta Carreri during her voyage to the Upper Volta (today Burkina Faso) in June 1982. My collaboration with Roberta began like this, transcribing onto computer a typewritten copy of this travel diary. In reality, when I did this in January 2006 I did not know anything about the book that Roberta had already started writing. The interest and curiosity that these pages elicited in me was the motivation that guided and pushed me during the period of our work together.

So, with regard to the paradoxical logic that has inspired the writing of this book, I take advantage of the privilege that the last page allows me by quoting one of the pages that have been 'wasted'. After all, Roberta quotes T.S. Eliot in the same travel diary: 'What we call the beginning is often the end / And to make an end is to make a beginning. / The end is where we start from.' Even for me, therefore, the beginning of my work will also be its end.

I see the great baobab trees reaching out towards the sky which, as tradition would have it, are its roots. It is said here that all things on earth have fallen from the sky. The baobab is a tree that has fallen head first. Its roots are the residence of the souls of the dead.

During a pause we stop not far away from one of these baobab trees and I ask Mette to take a photograph.[2] *It is impossible to reach its branches, which start to sprout twenty metres above the ground, so I satisfy myself by climbing up its roots and insert myself in a cranny of its trunk. The branches are the roots, the roots are the branches.*

How many souls of the dead live in that baobab?

May the words of this book, whose roots sink deep in the earth of experience, keep the constant aspiration of its branches to reach out, infinitely, towards the sky. A sky not only for and by itself.

Rome, December 2006

Notes

1 See Chapters 20, 23 and 25 in this book.
2 Mette Bovin is the Danish anthropologist who suggested the voyage to Africa. The second part of Chapter 10 deals with this journey.

31 Backward steps
Epilogue by Nando Taviani

I could wish the author and her book the best of luck, praising the actress. If I were a professional writer of epilogues – like the 'peaceful' spectators of one time – I would hold a glass in one hand and with the other lift the new volume in full view. I would caress the cover, speak easily about its good qualities and mention a little flaw in passing, just to give the impression of an objective assessment. By doing so I could stimulate readers to an informed and engaged re-reading, and maybe provide them with one of those sidelong glances that give the illusion of intelligence. I could well pose for one of those arm-in-arm photographs that show how well we understand each other, the author and I.

Instead I will take a couple of steps backward and start with the story of Madam Pauline in Mexico, where the relationship between actors and spectators, within and beyond a mirror, is thorny, asymmetrical and misunderstood. Mirrors do not lie, but they do invert.

Once upon a time, on one of the concluding carnival nights of 1840, there was a magnificent theatre in Mexico City. Madam Pauline, star singer and dancer with a French prose and music company, was performing there for the first time. She made a triumphant stage entrance, dancing splendidly. At the end of a masterfully executed series of pirouettes (with her rich skirt blowing up like a balloon), Pauline stood still at the centre of the stage, on tiptoes and with her arms arched above her head. She waited expectantly for the applause. What she got instead was an ice-cold reception, much worse than boos. She stood there in precarious balance, quivering and furious, in checkmate. The spectators sat, almost cold-blooded, in front of her.

Pauline anecdote.

Madam Pauline and her company had only just arrived in that theatre. They came from Paris and must have said to themselves: 'Let's go and conquer Mexico!' They wanted to overwhelm the spectators there with good taste, with the art of living well, and with the sparkling cream of civilisation and Europe: sex and smiles, exciting music, and stories of twisted love exhibited for laughs, without any melodramatic violence. So Madam Pauline decided to present herself to her best and most elegant advantage on stage: with a new and beautiful dress. Although she did not expect to find a suitable gown in that backwater of a country in the nineteenth century, she went to a local dressmaker. It so happened that the seamstress had the right dress for her, and though it was not for sale, it was waiting for a special occasion. The dressmaker said she would gladly surrender the gown to the foreign Parisian actress. She also said that it was worth a fortune, but she would charge a special price. It was made of the finest lace, with intricate embroidery and satin flakes of gold quilting holding the drapery of the skirt at regular intervals.

Madam Pauline had never seen a dress like it before, not even in Paris. She bought it on the credit of the imminent box office takings: a few adjustments and it would seem as if it were made to measure. The ladies in the theatre boxes would be dressed up to the nines on opening night, but they would not know what a true lady, a true prima donna, looked like until she, Pauline, went on stage. They would savour the nostalgia of Europe and the theatre because she would know how to breathe life into that rich and magnificent dress, transforming it into a phantasmagoria. She knew what she had to do. She rehearsed. She planned and foresaw the astonishment of the public.

But not *that* kind of astonishment.

Stunned by her cold reception, she lowered herself from tiptoes (she had to do imperceptible little steps not to give the impression that she was moving), and rested in the first position. She then lowered her arms. Sometimes applause bursts after some seconds' delay. This is the best. She waited, but she soon realised that it was to no avail. Then something unexpected blew up on the other side of the footlights: a wave of disapproval, superiority and disgust. The wave broke in a hundred murmurs, galloping between deep bouts of whispered discussions, gesticulations, up and down between the boxes and the stalls. The female members of the audience were especially busy, while fathers, husbands, brothers, friends, admirers and fiancés interrupted the ladies to tell them not to interrupt. The performance continued, but there was no way it could be brought back on an even keel – it was shipwrecked on indifference. Not because the spectators were apathetic – on the contrary, they were wide awake and active, very talkative, but among each other. A new drama was taking place, and the spectators themselves were playing it: the actors did not have a clue. It was a nightmare.

You have to know that a month earlier (before the famous Parisian company arrived), a young and beautiful newlywed countess died in Mexico City. She was much loved. Her tragedy had moved everyone: they found her dead one morning, without a reason or prior illness. They dressed her up in her bridal dress for her funeral. The uncovered corpse was paraded through the streets, which were all filled with weeping mourners. She seemed to be fast asleep, pale, serene and beautiful in her majestic dress. And that's how she was buried in the family chapel.

But the precious dress of that young bride was exhumed from the grave and passed from one dealer to another until it reached the back shop of that dressmaker, who, instead of sending it far away, had the thoughtless idea of selling it in situ to the foreign actress. Pauline's astonishing entrée, extremely elegant and fascinating in its own right, was transformed for the spectators into the disgusting self-confession of a graverobber. After this scandal, the custom of undressing the corpses of the rich before burial prevailed in Mexico City in order not to tempt gravediggers and sextons. *No hay mal que por bien no venga.*

The story comes down to us as narrated by a spectator, Madam Frances Calderón de la Barca, an American from Boston who was married to the Spanish ambassador (her maiden name was Frances Erskine Inglis). She stayed in Mexico City for a couple of years only, from 1839 to 1842. On her return to Boston she published *Life in Mexico* in 1843, containing fifty-three letters from a provincial and slightly uncivilised capital. Among her friends in Boston we find the half-blind William H. Prescott (who published the great historic portrait *The Conquest of Mexico*, also in 1843), Longfellow, Emerson and Hawthorne. After hearing the story of Madam Pauline, the latter was heard to exclaim: 'What a seductive tragedy!'

Madam Calderón de la Barca, formerly Lady Frances Erskine Inglis, was quite perplexed: what tragedy? It was rather funny to her. And 'seductive'? The stench of death still lingered in that dress! Her writer friend replied: 'Tragedy, my lady, a big tragedy. The forever unfulfilled Eros of Tragedy.'

Maybe.

In fact, it cannot be said that everyone saw the event like the spouse of the Spanish ambassador from her theatre box (and most of the other spectators with her) – that is, as an exhilarating and atrocious joke hatched on the spur of the moment. Perhaps for at least one spectator in that theatre at the conclusion of the 1840 carnival, there did indeed appear the quintessence of seductive tragedy that Hawthorne talked about. On seeing Pauline dancing her way onto the stage, one of the spectators, perhaps alone while the rest began their clamour, may really have enjoyed the sight and surprise of a born-again corpse with gaiety written all over her face. This spectator could really have contemplated – with a sense of horror and release, and to the rhythm of the light music with its gentle and determined steps – something like joy *that she wants to take you with her.*

End of anecdote.

I have recalled this anecdote because it always seemed to me an emblem of theatre and mirrors, and also because it involves humble things, *qui pro quo*, and dressmaking.

Why did the author-actress of this book ask me to write the epilogue? Why didn't she ask an actor?

In spite of good will, reciprocal respect, admiration and affection, when a spectator and an actor talk about what happened between them – the performance – there are bound to be mishaps. 'But how could you not understand? Did you not see?' the actor asks the spectator. 'But did you really not want me to understand what I saw?' the spectator replies. Generally speaking, it is best not to proceed with the discussion at this point. In a few moves one risks ending up with the most insipid and sad commonplaces of theatre. 'Ah, spectators – I don't know where they come up with certain ideas,' actors say to one another, shaking their heads. And some actors would add: 'They don't have any eyes. They only see what they think.' In turn, spectators also shake their heads, saying: 'Actors? They're clever as long they're on stage, but the moment they're off it you realise that they do not have a clue! They do, but they do not understand.'

How sad. Such judgements are so out of place.

The differences are due to geometry, and the mishaps are the other side of the confusion that makes the relationship between actor and spectator such a rich and vibrant one. We have different points of view, which are not always contrasting but which are fatal mirror images of each other. Mirrors *appear* to be good and honest because they do not show the image upside down, they do not deform it – even though they invert right and left. It is exactly for this reason that they are interesting, a source of games and predictions, but they are never innocent. At times they are abominable.

It can be said that the unease of mirrors sharpens the value of theatre to the same extent that it creates a source of misunderstandings. It can also be said that books such as this, where a theatre professional takes on the responsibility to speak in the first person, resist that unease in the attempt to 'translate into written words the core of a professional life that I have chosen in order to escape the ambiguity of words', as the writer herself says on the final page of the book.

For sartorial reasons, the author of this book once reacted as if she wanted to hit me. She was joking, of course, but I automatically took a step backward: the energy was the same. 'What are you saying?! A cheap little dress? Do you know how much it cost, this cheap little dressing gown, as you call it? Don't you realise how elegant this dress is?' I did not realise. And yet...

As so often happens at the end of a cheerful dinner, when fellow diners, partly out of jest and partly out of spite, bombard each other with pellets of crumbs, she kept throwing information at me: where she bought the elegant dress (from who knows which good shop in Milan), how much she paid for it (a lot), which design, which fabric. For me it looked like what is sometimes called a charwoman's dress. What's worse, it still looks like that to me every time I see Roberta Carreri's performance in the work demonstration *The Whispering Winds in Theatre and Dance*, to which she hardly refers in this book.

When she stands up from her chair, where she has been waiting her turn, Carreri the actress carries a small box (or rather, an elegant suitcase) with her. She wears what I mistook for 'a cheap little dressing gown'. Then, in the course of her presentation (some twenty minutes long), she takes out other clothes from the suitcase and puts them on. At the end she wears a veil and a long and heavy winter dress in the style of an early twentieth-century lady. It is a very elegant dress, black and classy. She says a text by Joyce, Molly Bloom's. Is it, perhaps, because of the intended contrast with the final image of the attractive lady in a luxurious garment, that I saw and continue to see the stylish little dress of the beginning (light and very modern with a hint of youth) as shabby and cheap?

It is not important. It is just a little misunderstanding. There are others. I will come back to these later on, like a leitmotif.

For actors, the performance is a point of arrival. For spectators, it is a point of departure.

Actors have the luxury of double vision when they are performing. They can see all that is happening around them at the moment of its occurrence. They can also see, internally, the river of the performance as a whole: what has been and what shall be. Pastpresentfuture. The remains of the choices that led them to the result can be found sedimented in the subterranean recesses of their memory, the various stories, the forgotten drafts. The actress knows (even if she perhaps thinks she does not remember) where that particular movement came from, how many other movements she had to delete before arriving at the one she does now. She knows where her costume comes from, how she chose it, and how many she rejected.

The better a performance is, the more alive is its relationship with the spectators. The more it disorientates or even shakes the spectator, the more misunderstandings are likely to flourish. There is a way of making the communication innocuous, devoid of any misunderstandings: all you have to do is show what needs to be understood and nothing else, avoiding stimulating further the senses and the imagination of who is watching. But then the relationship between actors and spectators ends up in a contrasting separation. A spectator who understands everything is soon bored. Without mirrors, they are patient for a while, but then they get annoyed or even angry at the actors for boring them, as if the actors were doing this on purpose specifically to bore them. Or else, if they have a comfortable seat, they might sink into their own personal thoughts. In the luckier cases, they may simply fall asleep.

It seems to me that misunderstandings are the very salt of theatre. If the relationship is charged with meaning and is alive, is this due to the dialectic of mutual misunderstanding that animates it?

I am not saying that the spectator always and systematically understands everything in reverse, or that the actor is not aware of the spectator's perspective on what is happening on stage. Almost always the actor thinks of this – and how. Actors know this, and they know that they know. But not in everything, or for everything. The most effective part of the actor's presence always triggers an association of ideas and impulses in the minds of observers that move in ways that the actor cannot anticipate. In fact, every spectator has his or her own subtexts. Spectators err if they assume that this actor or that actress had the intention of making them see everything that they saw. Once this memory consolidates, it is difficult to change it. It becomes a veritable object. It has all the subjective characteristics of what we call 'objective'.

We can even say that in theatre, we see as if we already remember. We can equally say that anyone who acts behaves as if they are continually gambling on the meaning that their intentions acquire in the eyes of those who observe the actions. Is theatrical communication, when it is well formed, a game of chance?

It is not words that are ambiguous, but relationships – all of them, and by their nature.

When I was young I could bark quite well. One of my jokes during summer holiday evenings by the sea consisted of barking and howling. All of a sudden all the dogs in the neighbourhood would answer back, much to the alarm of other people and the amusement of my friends. 'Be careful,' one of my mates told me once, 'that the dogs don't understand something you don't mean when you bark!' He was a cautious type. 'Suppose you send them a message and don't understand its meaning, but they, the dogs, understand it, and suppose you piss them off, and suppose they come after us, what shall we do then?'

Those who act also send messages to the dogs – and quite a few metaphorical dogs can be found hiding among spectators. Due to this, the best and the worst things happen in theatre. In daily life, misunderstandings are disagreeable. In theatre, they can be the basis of pleasure, intelligence, and sometimes discovery. They enable the experience of an experience.

This does not depend only on talent, grace or inspiration on the part of those who act the performance, and not only on intelligent deciphering on the part of those who observe. There is something other. And this something other, if not quite a grammar, has a basic level of know-how.

The book in front of us, written by an actress, gambles on the possibility of transmitting at least some clues about this knowledge.

We have just finished reading and examining this book. We hoped to grasp *how it's done*. There is a lot of technique in these pages, techniques of rhythms and of forms. But have we really *grasped them*? There is even autobiography, and autobiography – as we know – however sincere, is the least 'true', in the sense that we consider true what we consider to be objective. Not even technical information and explanations are objective. They limit themselves to seeming so. When an artisan or an artist explains how they reach results, when they speak about how they elaborate forms, it seems as if they are tracing a map. But this is not geography: it is history. They are always stories, even when they put on the guise of an instruction manual and the peremptory concision of a recipe.

Neither the autobiography nor the technical indications stay fixed in their place. They are continually overflowing each other's riverbeds. In their mix they do not serve to *grasp* anything, but they do allow something to be touched by a finger. Immediately afterwards, they force you to take a step backward.

Perhaps the source of interest for books such as the one we have just finished reading is for their traces and their snow. They make us walk backwards, in the opposite direction to the one we face as spectators when we rush forward in our thoughts, appreciations and criticisms: our *reflections*. Backward steps take us back to the flavour and value of first steps, those that oversee the elementary paradox of the theatre, its *mortal* sin according to the ancient moralists, its *mortal* leap (somersault) according to us: that is, to voluntarily see other human beings who voluntarily act to make us see ourselves, in a mirror relationship that is materially based on inversion and ambiguity. Their left is our right and vice versa, both in the literal sense and above all in the figurative sense. They compose statues, which they transform in music. We, the spectators, see 'music in figures', which we then remember as image and sculpture. The passage from sculpture to music was the subject of the thesis Roberta Carreri thought of writing before she switched over to the side of the actors.

Touching with a finger does not mean that one knows (almost) nothing. It is the only way of getting to know the flavour of otherness. (The moment you touch something with the hand, with the entire hand, the flavour of otherness unknown to you is dispersed. You go back to recognising your old hand, its grip, and not the immanence of a relationship, an ambiguous tie).

On second thoughts, theatrical experience can be condensed in a few words: *there's something else*.

The author of this book has named this, after some hesitation, *Traces*. In what sense? There are traces that are wiped out to prevent us from being reached. There are traces like when Father Brown broke a window with an umbrella and left a trail of similar ruses so he could be tracked down. There are traces like the remains of people who have passed away. And there are traces that give the impression that 'something' has happened although it is no longer there, like nuclear physics. There are traces like footprints that can be stepped in again, and there are traces that are left behind to lead followers astray. There is also a trace that is like the outline of a speech, or in the sense of minimum quantities, which are not measurable but are still significant, like 'trace substances' in chemical analysis.

The expedient on which Roberta Carreri has built this mirror-book consists in the oscillation between autobiographical pages, work diaries and technical details. A similar oscillation also organises the work demonstration *Traces in the Snow*. The same expedient craftsmanship supports her performance in *The Whispering Winds in Theatre and Dance*, which, as I have already mentioned, is hardly mentioned in this book. Even this performance aims at complexity by means of disarming simplicity. Professional recipes, one's own person, and some characters:

three traces. It is understood that two would not be enough. They would not have been sufficient to disarm conditioned reflexes.

I have seen *The Whispering Winds* work demonstration various times, ever since it appeared fresh and unexpected in public during the 1996 Copenhagen ISTA session dedicated to the links between theatre and dance. I think that at the time nobody, neither the actors nor their director, thought the demonstration was worth keeping. It was scheduled as a one-time intervention, a kind of round-table presentation by three actresses and one actor of Odin, each showing their individual conceptions of the opposition and identity between theatre and dance. In addition to words, the four interlocutors also used the costume of one or more characters. What came out of this, to the surprise of even Eugenio Barba himself, was a ready-made work – an ironic, witty and concise scenic pamphlet, a distilled dose of theatrical knowledge. It remained in the repertory of Odin, and they still present it today.

The Whispering Winds contains four performances in this order: Julia Varley, Roberta Carreri, Iben Nagel Rasmussen and Torgeir Wethal.[1] They are accompanied on the accordion, guitar and violin by Kai Bredholt, Jan Ferslev and Frans Winther. The second performance, by the author of this book, seems disconcertingly simple because it aims directly at the spectators' heads and in part disarms them. It exposes and makes palpable that which works in the liminal areas of each brain.

She arrives wearing her 'little dress', puts down the coloured suitcase she carries with her, leans against it on the floor as if it were the headboard of a sofa, and begins to tell her story. She says that since her first steps as an actress, dance and theatre were the other side of each other. She does not speak as if she is giving a lecture or addressing a conference. She acts. She uses appropriate and precise tones and movements according to the design of a well-made scenic score. Then she stops talking, the music begins, and she dances. We realise (we had been forewarned, otherwise most of us would not have realised) that the design of the movements is repeated, dilated here and there, but essentially the same. We see that the physical actions, which initially seemed to be made for the words, preserve their form and their independent consistency in direct relation to the music. She 'interrupts' (*spezza*) the music while still following it. On top of the little and light modern dress, the actress puts on a heavy dress from another epoch. She transforms herself into an attractive lady, more words follow, and the same score is repeated, this time to give life to the monologue of Molly Bloom.

It has also been explained to us that this sequence or that score of actions come from a distant relationship with other figures and stories, far removed from the one we see: the iconography of the Magdalene at the foot of the Cross. But maybe I am wrong and I am superimposing different information. Perhaps in this case the score was originally composed on the basis of what we see at the end, the monologue of Molly Bloom. It does not matter. What matters is that the actions and intonations, which are heterogeneous in origin and which remain the same, adapt perfectly every time to the different words or to the music with which they dance. While we feel and test them with the eyes, it seems like they belong only to the relationship in which we see them at the time. The terms of the relationship change, and yet each time the congruence of the form and its meaning appears to be made specifically and necessarily for that instant. Is it virtuosity? A trick?

It is the exposure of a fundamental and living cell of theatre, as if observed under the lens of a powerful microscope. This is how the *facts* of the scene thicken, how the goldsmith's action becomes flesh and meaning in our minds; this is how its identity can change from day to night, while the dynamism that gives it shape and life remains immutable. We realise – we knew well enough, but now we realise – that in reality our mind works at least as much as the actress. In it grows the congruence between gesture and word, movement and music; a congruence that is coloured like something unique and unitary, which we interpret, judge and metabolise as an inseparable all-in-one. Actually we *realise* because our sight *corrects* certain thought-automatisms we have regarding the point-by-point dependence between the line of physical action and the musical score or music. The microscope shows that the different points of the two lines react to and fuse into one another, but they are not born from each other. This unity is the result of a judicious coupling: it is a 'one' that is born from 'two', from the diversity and from the autonomous and precise internal coherence of two separate and separable compositions. Therefore they give birth, so to speak, to indissoluble and dissimilar unities; incomparable, if they had not been compared directly and repeatedly, one after the other in front of our eyes. What allows them to propagate differently is the precision that makes them autonomous.

Now let us see what happens: we have only just realised, and we already think we have touched (by hand) how the whole thing works. It is not true: we have only barely touched with a finger. A petulant little voice in our mind says: 'It is clear! I know how to do it!' It is not true. Try it and you will see. Try to do it and you will find yourself with a cold little body of an exercise that serves for nothing. It is better to take a step backward.

It is enough to take only a couple of steps backward, just about the distance of a little common sense, to realise that the exercise is exercised to make it stop being an exercise, and that the work demonstration is effective for its reverse: the work of demonstration. It seems as if it is made up of indications, but in reality, when it works, it condenses a knot of paths, and while saying one thing it does something else. It says, 'See how it is made?' and then does something that would not make any sense repeating. It is a weave that takes you round in circles, until when it is right, almost by chance, you touch with a finger.

What?

Sometimes seeing, seeing immediately again and yet again is a way of catching in brief the sense of a long professional process, of a biography, and ultimately of a *person*.

Some of us may have had the good fortune to meet one of those artisans or artists, masters or teachers who, if asked how they learn a difficult technical knot, would not answer but simply show it to you, again and again. But we already know that they can do it. What we want to know is *how* it is done, as if seeing it is enough to understand it. We want them to explain it to us. But they do not explain anything: rather, they do it again, showing you the folds. They do not talk or speak of anything else, and in the meanwhile they repeat, repeat and repeat, changing the rhythm, changing the speed. Sometimes they are focussed, and at other times they seem distracted. Now they appear afraid of not being able to do it, and then they enjoy repeating it. They show you the difficulty, and then they exhibit aristocratic *sprezzatura*.[2] They half-smile with their eyes, as if to say how easy it is – which is not at all the case. You have new questions to ask, but by now you realise that they would fall on deaf ears.

What do they show you, in fact?

Certainly not how clever they are (we already know that). And not that they are one of those for whom silence is golden (we have already understood that only too well). And not that they like to take you for a ride (we half-suspect this, but they are too obliging to tease you). Are they perhaps telling you that you need something else, and that, anyway, even if you found the secret, you would never learn in the little time you have available? They are telling you a lot of things simultaneously. That is why they keep their mouths shut. Patience is needed. They show you the knot, the technique, the agility, the length of training, and together with the mental-physical attitude, the coexistence of commitment and disinterest, of fun and work, of devotion and self-mockery. They show you the distinctive strength of mind that allows them to spend a great part of their lives on miniscule and infinitesimal things that are enormously difficult, and hugely useless until that moment in which they succeed to liberate from themselves a kind of radioactivity that makes a clean slate of the technique and exercise to materialise an image, an unburied shadow, that was previously not there, not even as a prediction. Not always. Not in any case. Not certainly. It depends.

At first one gropes in the dark – the darkness of a thousand precisions.

Do you remember those moments of panic as a child when they made you put on clothing that had to pass over the head, and for a second you felt like suffocating, entangled as you were in the darkness of the garment? Then the hands found their way out of the sleeves, and the face resurfaced in the light with a smile that held a microscopic hint of panic. That is how the elegant lady emerges from the dress at the end of Roberta Carreri's performance, with that childlike trace on her face, while she concludes the dance of her costume. In the course of a brief performance during an ensemble demonstration, next to the actress, to her dance and to her character, the shadow lengthens at the end. We can catch a glimpse of it. The stillness that comes after the monologue is the slightly convex calm from which – in maritime novels – the backs of monsters and whales emerge silently. The calmness of an attractive lady whose monsters are sensible enough to swim in the deep. How is it that I risk being moved by it? Wasn't it supposed to be just a technical demonstration?

The demonstration is over. We are at the theatre.

The theatre is not an art of images, as we so often offhandedly repeat. It is so, but only in part, maybe ninety or ninety-five percent. However, what ultimately counts is the rest: the art of an image that disappears the instant you see it. The sense of disappearance. An aesthetic? Definitely. But it is a terribly shaken up aesthetic, one that is constructed in the same moment it gives shape to its disappearance. One that is constructed as it dissipates.

In the book, Roberta Carreri often speaks of the performance *Judith*. One evening I happened to see it simultaneously in its own space and in its own mirror. There were a hundred or so people present, but only a few of us had, by chance, the privilege of a real mirror at our disposal. If the eyes of the actress had fallen on me in the course of her performance that evening, she would have been dangerously irritated with me – and rightly so. I was a distracted spectator. For half of the time I did not look at her, but out of the window.

We were in a big dining hall at a seaside holiday camp in Salento where the fifth session of ISTA was taking place in early September 1987. There *Judith* was presented in one of its first performances. The dining hall had enormous windows overlooking the sea. It was evening, and due to the darkness outside the windows became mirrors. In this way I had double vision: the performance in front of me and, just to its right, its reflected image, well-defined and in lateral perspective. From that angle, the image of the performance appeared polished like a film: mobile statuary with authoritative frames. The clarity and sharpness of the reflected image seemed to wear away when I looked at the live performance in flesh and blood. Crumbling a bit, as it got mixed with the impurity of breath and of the veil of sweat; with the veins of the neck, the forehead, the hands, the shins; with the noise of the feet on the floor; with the chance nature of my point of view, my rhythms of attention, my blinking and at times misting eyes. In contrast, the reflected performance appeared like painted images in the glass. Much to my amazement I realised that, unknowingly, I was thinking and watching in reverse: the reflection appeared to be the original. I surprised myself (like a child who still deceives himself that he is the one who chooses) by asking what I wanted to choose: the theatre, or the aesthetic of the glass? Then, while the theatre in front of my eyes went on, I suffered two or three knocks.

I said to myself: that is why I am here.

There is a person, despite oneself, behind every person. Someone we never see. Someone who is least of all willed by the person to whom they belong (or from whom they emanate). But in theatre, sometimes, there appears a little opening. Something that shakes the shape. Because it cannot manifest itself in a natural way, it needs an extraneous and artificial shape. It needs form to shake it. That is what the form is there for: not to be admired, but to be shaken. Shaking it, the exhumed person shakes the spectator. But who or what it is that shakes the spectator, and whether it is in a position to do so, depends. All the rest (technique, know-how) is very important – but it *depends*. That is why theatre remains, deep down, a form of play, *gioco, jeu, spiel*: a gamble. A game of chance – and also of courage.

Years later, the gift of a real mirror was offered to every spectator. In *Andersen's Dream*, the ceiling of the little amphitheatre in which both actors and spectators are gathered is indeed a mirror. The floor is full of footprints and snow. At one point Roberta Carreri makes up her face as an old lady, leans on a walking stick, and does a strip-tease.

Seen up there, in the cleanliness of the mirror, it is a very funny scene. Seen directly from below, in the live impurity of presence, it also possesses bitterness, that thorny feeling which comes from the union of composition and unseemliness. This is what constitutes true art, if we want to use this terminology: beauty free from good taste.

In a later scene, all the actors appear wearing pyjamas as if they are going to bed. Each of them carries their own photograph printed on long, thin sheets of paper. They unroll them and it is really them, in costume, life-size portraits in black and white. Some show them off. Others hold them in their arms like cuddling a baby. Then they spread out their images on a big bed, or a bier, where they are slowly consumed by fire.

Death? For some of us, our heart seemed to ache. It seemed like the actors were daring a bit too much, like drawing bad luck upon themselves while the music evoked a sweet evening wind. My old spectator's empty head was filled with ideas it did not want to think about, neither for myself nor for my dear friends on stage.

Oh yes, spectators do get some fancy ideas sometimes that make you wonder where they get them from. But which death? It is only (or absolutely) the quintessence of theatre that makes an art out of the sense of disappearance and passing away. When you look, you are aware that what you are seeing – exactly as you see it now and as you want to fix it with your eyes – is already passing away. Remove this anxiety about disappearance, and you will only have a video in your hands.

In the breeze of passing away, it would indeed be foolish to argue who is right and who is wrong.

I thought that I could use the Indian word 'Syadvada' as the title of this epilogue. I wrote the title at the top of the first page, on the first line, and it made me laugh. First of all because the Jianistic Indian term sounded pompous, but above all because it is practically untranslatable in the West: 'uncertainty', 'dubious', 'ambiguity', 'relativism', asceticism'? And even here 'Syadvada' is only very remotely similar to these words. It means something else. A less faithful translation might say 'perhapsity'. An improbable word. 'Backward steps' is better.

And yet it is exactly from *perhapsity* that, without any pomp, theatre makes craftsmanship and sometimes art. In fact, as soon as it swells a little and lifts from the ground, it becomes a con man's praise.

I like the way this book is written, between information, notes from work diaries, photos and brief autobiographical comments, in a style that sometimes seems concerned with its rendition. It does not only speak about theatre (as we usually do); it also preserves its traces (as so rarely happens).

And so, if I were a professional writer of epilogues, I might lift my elbow and risk proposing a toast directly to the author. I would tell her, I suppose, not to worry about her book, that words are ambiguous and betray *reality*, the warmth of experience which makes one feel whole. Because this *reality* – I would tell her – does not really exist at all. Yours are good and precious words. They are uncertain gambles, of course, like every other trace. Even 'experiences', when still being experimented with, are changeable traces, warmer and apparently *truer*, but they impetuously change the form and content of our internal language. Traces set on paper and in words change slower than others, and sometimes they last much longer than the person who writes them: that is why they appear particularly unfaithful and always very cold to us, compared with what changes so rapidly and generates warmth in that speed. By a strange and shared illusion, all that is warm seems to us to be truer. Just as footprints that are quickly undone in snow appear warmer than those on solid land, which sometimes remain intact for weeks and in some cases for centuries, frozen in stone. Warm and cold are indeed very different, but not when it comes to distinguishing between the true and the less true.

Reality – I feel – is something else. It is what we try to run away from, one backward step after another, from birth to the end. In this run we are alive. What else could 'reality' mean, if not the senseless jaws of a wolf? Whence does it come – from which seduction, from which self-destructive impatience – this desire to escape the blessed precarious unreality of fiction and words?

And so I do want to make a toast, to wish you and your book the best of luck. But no, I will not wish you the usual *in bocca al lupo*.[3]

Notes

1 Translator's note: for details about changes in the actors' line up in this work demonstration, see footnote 2 in Chapter 25 in Carreri's text.
2 Translator's note: *sprezzatura* is a complex Italian term that refers to the art of making the difficult look easy.
3 Translator's note: the literal meaning of *in bocca al lupo* is 'in the mouth of the wolf'; its figurative meaning is 'good luck'.

Index

Alves, Patricia 93
Anabasis 46, 122
Andersen's Dream 130, 137–38, 145–46, 158, 227
Azuma, Katsuko 70, 102, 106, 109

Bacci, Roberto 11
The Book of Dances 17, 21, 71
Bovin, Mette 52, 214
Brie, César 93
Butoh 105, 111–14
Brecht's Ashes 22, 69, 84, 88–92, 95, 130, 159
Brecht, Bertolt 88–89, 116, 130
Bredholt, Kai 94, 223

Carpignano Salentino 14–19, 44, 69, 71, 94, 127, 159
Carreri Pardeilhan, Alice 44–45, 92, 95–97, 100, 111, 115
Chierichetti, Beppe 7, 15
Christensen, Jens 9
Christiansen, Ragnar 10
Cieślak, Ryszard 27
The Chronic Life 145–57
Come! And the day will be ours 17, 21, 46, 69, 83, 98, 114, 130
composition 20, 32–36, 57, 58, 92, 204, 228
Cots, Toni 21

dynamic immobility 23, 84, 102, 191, 193–94, 205, 207

'The Dance of Intentions' xvii, 23, 68, 183ff

extroversion 37–41, 58

Ferai 129
Ferslev, Jan 93, 135–43, 223
Fiskedam 88, 89, 92
Fjordefalk, Tom 114
Floris, Elena 12, 134

Geronimo 46–52, 122, 158
The Gospel According to Oxyrhincus 84, 89, 96–97, 98–99, 112, 122, 130, 213
Grotowski, Jerzy xiv, 8, 20, 28, 85, 127, 156

Hijikata, Tatsumi 110, 111

Judith 111–17, 121–22, 131–32, 137, 158, 226–27

Iaiza, Raúl 143, 146
introversion 37–41, 58

Kaosmos 69, 118, 121–26, 130, 152, 213
Kaspariana 129
Kitt, Donald 146
Knudsen, Knud Erik 48
kokoro 109, 115
Kongshaug, Jesper 150, 156

Kvamme, Elsa 44

Larsen, Tage 10, 18, 22, 28, 48, 94, 122, 130, 146, 148
Laukvik, Else Marie 10, 18, 20, 21, 44, 89, 94, 159
Lindh, Ingemar xviii, 3

The Million 22, 69, 88, 95, 102
Min Fars Hus 8–11, 14, 129, 147, 160
Mythos 70, 130, 131, 137

Nakajima, Natsu 105, 109, 111
Nielsen, Tina 21, 146
Nihon Buyo 59, 70, 102, 106

Odissi 11, 102, 104
Ohno, Katsuo 108–10
Omolú, Augusto 126, 134, 143

Paglialunga, Rina 93, 94
Panigrahi, Sanjukta 102, 104
Pardeilhan, Francis 21, 44, 47, 48, 92, 93–97
Pompa, Pierangelo 146
Pro, Fausto 146

Quang Hai, Tran 131

Rasmussen, Iben Nagel xv, 9–11, 14–19, 21, 23, 27, 42, 72, 78, 85, 93, 146, 160, 164, 223

Ricciardelli, Silvia 21, 46, 93

Salt 135–44, 213
Sats 27–28, 30, 33, 57, 68, 188, 189, 207
Skeel, Ulrik 10, 43, 93, 94
slow motion xv, 23, 29–31, 158, 194–96
the snake 23, 189–90, 193, 194, 204–06
Ström, Odd 16, 18
Stigsgaard, Anna 146

Tabucchi, Antonio 137, 141
Talabot 97, 115
Taviani, Nando 16, 24, 146
Teatro Tascabile di Bergamo 7–11
Theatrum Mundi 104
Torp, Jan 18, 21, 46

Varley, Julia 21, 223
Vescovi, Renzo 7–8
Vetter, Michael 131

Wethal, Torgeir xv, 10, 11, 14, 18, 20, 24, 27, 29, 44, 85, 89, 93–97, 111, 118, 130, 145–57, 159, 184, 223
Winther, Frans 153, 223
Woolf, Ana 146, 152, 155

Ybema, Walter 94

eBooks
from Taylor & Francis

Helping you to choose the right eBooks for your Library

Add to your library's digital collection today with Taylor & Francis eBooks. We have over 45,000 eBooks in the Humanities, Social Sciences, Behavioural Sciences, Built Environment and Law, from leading imprints, including Routledge, Focal Press and Psychology Press.

Choose from a range of subject packages or create your own!

Benefits for you
- Free MARC records
- COUNTER-compliant usage statistics
- Flexible purchase and pricing options
- 70% approx of our eBooks are now DRM-free.

ORDER YOUR FREE INSTITUTIONAL TRIAL TODAY

Free Trials Available

We offer free trials to qualifying academic, corporate and government customers.

Benefits for your user
- Off-site, anytime access via Athens or referring URL
- Print or copy pages or chapters
- Full content search
- Bookmark, highlight and annotate text
- Access to thousands of pages of quality research at the click of a button.

eCollections
Choose from 20 different subject eCollections, including:

Asian Studies
Economics
Health Studies
Law
Middle East Studies

eFocus
We have 16 cutting-edge interdisciplinary collections, including:

Development Studies
The Environment
Islam
Korea
Urban Studies

For more information, pricing enquiries or to order a free trial, please contact your local sales team:

UK/Rest of World: **online.sales@tandf.co.uk**
USA/Canada/Latin America: **e-reference@taylorandfrancis.com**
East/Southeast Asia: **martin.jack@tandf.com.sg**
India: **journalsales@tandfindia.com**

www.tandfebooks.com

CPSIA information can be obtained
at www.ICGtesting.com
Printed in the USA
JSHW011511211219
3107JS00012B/113